Coaching to Solutions

A Manager's Toolkit for Performance Delivery

Carole Pemberton

ELSEVIER

AMSTERDAM • BOSTON • HEIDELBERG • LONDON • NEW YORK • OXFORD
PARIS • SAN DIEGO • SAN FRANCISCO • SINGAPORE • SYDNEY • TOKYO
Butterworth-Heinemann is an imprint of Elsevier

Butterworth-Heinemann is an imprint of Elsevier
Linacre House, Jordan Hill, Oxford OX2 8DP
30 Corporate Drive, Suite 400, Burlington, MA 01803

First edition 2006

British Library Cataloguing in Publication Data
A catalogue record for this book is available from the British Library

Library of Congress Catalog Number: 2005937838

ISBN–13: 978-0-7506-5742-6
ISBN–10: 0-7506-5742-1

For information on all Butterworth-Heinemann publications
visit our web site at http://books.elsevier.com

Typeset by Cepha Imaging Pvt. Ltd., India
Printed and bound in Great Britain by MPG Books Ltd, Cornwall

06 07 08 09 10   10 9 8 7 6 5 4 3 2 1

Contents

Foreword

Being a great manager requires that you get the best from your team. Using coaching skills is undoubtedly the route to achieving that improved performance. But it is a particular skill that is distinct from other managerial responsibilities and fraught with role complications and confusions.

Carole Pemberton does a beautiful job of explaining, in clear and straightforward terms, the similarities, differences and overlaps. She shows you how to navigate your way through those different managerial responsibilities by placing coaching in its rightful context.

The next challenge is to develop those skills. So the author presents you with a truly integrated style of coaching, drawing from different psychological models, managerial expertise and coaching methods to create a model of coaching that is both simple and comprehensive.

With 30 years in the people development field I can see how skilfully she has woven together the theory and practice in such an accessible way that it will be really helpful to managers who are starting out on coaching and also to those who have experience. I have found some real gems of quotes, perspectives and powerful interventions that I will be adding to my practice.

This book is truly a treasure trove of ideas, models, practical interventions and to drive home the understanding, there are practical exercises for you to try out. There are copious case examples that explain in very down to earth terms how to utilise the skills and interventions. This is very important when you are trying to understand how to implement them back at work to find solutions to tricky people issues.

I am pleased to have been asked to write this foreword for I believe it is the best DIY book on coaching for managers on the market; and for training professionals responsible for organizational learning and development pro-grammes, this will prove to be an important resource for managing people performance.

John Leary-Joyce
CEO
Academy of Executive Coaching

Acknowledgements

This book is the product of the influences of the many individuals I have coached over the last twenty years. I cannot name you, but your responses have shaped the thinking from which this book came. Everything I have learnt as a coach has come from the opportunity to work with you. Coaching is the most privileged of activities, and I thank all those who have trusted me to help them become more of what they want to be.

I also thank the many managers I have worked with on development programmes. Managers who are committed to helping their staff achieve more, whilst not wanting to be defined as coaches. Your pragmatism and enthusiasm allowed me to test out my ideas and to learn from your feedback.

I am indebted to Evan George of the Brief Therapy Centre who gave me my first exposure to Solution Focused Therapy, and to the Academy of Executive Coaching who helped me to define my own model of coaching.

Particular thanks to Ailsa Marks, my commissioning editor, for her patience in encouraging me to write, as I procrastinated.

Finally, an enormous thank you to Bill and Cameron Dunn who accepted my absence from family life as I wrote, and to Eva Dugova for providing the childcare that made writing possible.

Introduction

If you have gone beyond looking at the cover of this book then it's likely you are already coaching, or there are expectations that you should. The growth of coaching has been a phenomenon of the last decade. Does that mean that it is new? No. Just as my granny would complain that no one had stress in her day but would frequently talk of friends who suffered from 'nerves', coaching has been around for as long as people have wanted to help others perform better. It may have been labelled teaching, instructing, guiding, supervising, giving a bit of help, but focus on what individuals did under that label and it is likely that we would see in many of them what is now being called coaching. Does it mean this is simply 'old wine in new bottles'? I don't believe so. The current focus on coaching is harnessing what has been learnt about the most valuable ways of helping individuals to deliver more effectively; ensuring their personal development is appropriate and helping individuals to better manage their careers.

What is particular about this book is that it has a strong focus on using what is known about helping individuals shift their attention away from problems, in order that they can find solutions that work for them. The coach's role is to enable the other person to find solutions, it is not to act as an analyst or a work-place therapist.

There is much in this book that you could already have discovered through experiences outside of work, but have never considered from the perspective of its value within work. Anyone who has experience of children, who has animals or who has been involved in a relationship already knows a good deal that will help them in coaching staff. Even if the responsibility of coaching others is a new one recently added into your objectives, you know more than you think you know. The purpose of this book is to highlight what you know and to add to it, so that your effectiveness in helping others is enhanced.

The book offers a structure for making your interactions with staff more powerful, and more likely to lead to action – as distinct from having enjoyable conversations that have no visible result. You may have discovered that for some staff who offer appreciative noises about how much they value your support and listening ear, support simply leads to dependence rather than independence. A cycle is created where they want your time, you work hard to provide answers to their issues in the hope they will reduce their demands, they express gratitude, ignore your advice and then ask for even more of your time. This is not coaching, this is rescuing without the coachee ever having to learn to swim. For most managers the motivation to coach is to help the other person to enhance their performance for mutual benefit, provided that it does not become a high-maintenance activity.

This book will not make you a life-coach, relationship coach, attraction coach, spiritual coach, well-being coach or any one of the hundreds of coaching niches that now exist. What it will do is help you deliver performance coaching within the daily demands of your role. It will equip you to coach during a five-minute conversation at someone's desk, in the corridor or any other place where you and your staff talk about work. You will not have to set aside hour-long slots labelled 'coaching', but your staff will know that what they are getting is different from normal daily interactions, even if they do not label it 'coaching'. You will know it is coaching, because you will see evidence of them taking responsibility for their actions, and will feel the burden of trying to come up with answers lifting.

This book is not intended for those who seek to be professional coaches, it is for those managers who either have had coaching assigned to them as a responsibility or who want to use their time with staff more effectively.

How to read the book

The case for coaching is the focus of Chapter 1. This allows you to consider the potential benefits of coaching as a means of raising the performance and motivation of staff.

Chapters 2 and 3 focus on what you already bring to coaching because of your life experiences, and how that can both help and get in the way of a coaching conversation.

Chapter 4 lays out the FAST coaching model and the STARTED structure for managing coaching conversations, so that any intervention, however short, has an outcome.

Chapter 5 begins the coaching process through laying out the skills of Setting Up the coaching conversation. These are Stage I skills.

Chapter 6 provides you with questions that will equip you to establish what is tangible in the situation. These questions are quantum questions because of the energy they provide in moving things forward.

Chapters 7 and 8 provide tools for dealing with assumptions held by the other person and for reality-checking their view of their situation. These three chapters form Stage II of the coaching conversation.

Chapter 9 moves you into Stage III of the conversation, when the shift is towards outcomes. Chapter 9 focuses on establishing the target for action.

Chapter 10 provides techniques that can be used to help the coachee find solutions that will address their target.

Chapter 11 deals with the reality of delivery. It moves you beyond the action plan to dealing with the issues that arise when someone tries to change a well-established behaviour. It acknowledges that the move to successful action is rarely smooth.

Chapter 12 links coaching to leadership and looks at the case for coaching from the perspective of the manager.

You are not required to read all the chapters sequentially. You may find that particular chapters are helpful in dealing with particular problems you are facing in coaching staff, and start with those.

For anyone who has yet to coach staff, it makes sense to follow the format of the book, so that the logic of the approach is made clear.

Whether you are new to coaching or have been coaching for some while, the chapters on looking at yourself are valuable, since each one of us coaches others based on what we have come to believe about human behaviour. Recognizing what those beliefs are helps us in recognizing why we do what we do, and when it may not be helpful to another person.

The book is subtitled 'a tool kit', and that is what it is intended to be. That is why each chapter offers alternative ways to help staff develop their performance, since no one way works for every individual. Each chapter is supported by case studies based on situations that arise within work, and exercises that you can use to develop your own coaching skills.

Use the book as a resource to aiding the performance development of others, and your own development as a leader who can coach quickly and effectively, wherever and whenever the opportunity arises.

1

Coaching –
why all the attention now?

In most cases people do not leave businesses. People leave managers.
Sir Clive Woodward

Twenty years ago, few people would have talked about coaching unless it related to sports performance. There it would have been recognized as a signal that the person had abilities that could be best developed through having focused attention on reducing technical weaknesses. Successful sportsmen would pay tribute to their coaches as key to achieving their goals. At the same time, to say to a manager, who would happily pay for tennis or golf coaching, that they needed a coach at work would have been seen as an insult. It would imply that they were underperforming, when career success rests on signalling to an employer that you are always performing to your full potential.

Move on to the 21st century and, for many business people to have an external coach has become a signal of success. It offers a safe space to talk about the loneliness of being near the top, lack of confidence, knowledge and skills gaps, the challenges of living the life of a senior manager, relationship difficulties with senior colleagues and even 'is it worth it?'. For an elite within organizations, external coaching is available as a source of support; a confidential relationship like no other within their working day. The sceptical have dismissed it as corporately sponsored therapy. The people who work as executive coaches come from a wide range of backgrounds, but they have often had extensive training to enable them to deal with the psychology of the individual interacting with the tough reality of a business environment.

For this very reason, many line managers resist the idea of being coaches to their staff. They believe that they do not have the skills to fulfil this remit, and they may have very little inclination. Their desire is to deliver on the objectives they have been set, applying the skills and motivation of their direct reports to support that delivery. Those who have an interest in coaching staff may hold back because they fear it will become a major part of their role, when in reality they have little spare capacity. They express concern that they will be dragged into areas that are beyond their competence, or that they will shift the focus of their relationship with staff to the 'touchy feely' when they need it to be focused on the 'doing quickly'.

All of this suggests that coaching is something that sits outside the 'real business' of getting the work done, and risks deflecting attention from delivery. I believe neither assertion is true, and that coaching is the most powerful enabler you have as a manager to gain what you need of an individual, and what they desire for themselves.

Regardless, however, of your own feelings about coaching, there is plentiful evidence that it has now become a necessary and required aspect of the manager's role.

The tipping point

In 2002 Malcolm Gladwell published *The Tipping Point*,[1] a hugely influential book that highlighted the ways in which ideas, products, music and fashions spread like viruses, to the point where they become embedded as part of a culture. What begins as an idea or fashion statement with appeal to a few can spread like an epidemic until it develops a 'stickiness' that glues it to its target audience. The universality of mobile phone use, the speed of iPod penetration, the focus on the eating habits of children, the rising acceptability of plastic surgery are all indicators of this viral spread. Coaching has been another. From an activity that would have been suppressed as a sign of deficit, it has come to be seen as a badge of success for those who have been identified as 'talent'. From an organizational perspective, it has also come to be seen as part of the management skill set that should be available to all direct reports.

In the Chartered Institute of Personnel and Development's (CIPD) survey of training and development activity in the UK,[2] 95 per cent reported that coaching had increased in their organizations in the last year. Even more significantly, 97 per cent agreed with the statement that coaching skills are a necessary part of a manager's skill set. The tipping point has been reached. Whether coaching is a good thing is now not even a subject for debate – it is a fact of life.

What is also true is that the person most likely to be delivering the coaching is someone like you: a busy overworked individual, who may well have received little or no training for this role. According to the CIPD study, only 5 per cent of organizations do not expect line managers to coach, but fewer than 20 per cent of organizations have trained all or most of their managers to deliver coaching. Regardless of your training, or lack of it, there is a ready audience within your direct reports. According to the CIPD, coaching is an organizational offer to two-thirds of junior and middle managers, and since 40 per cent of organizations report that they use no external coaches, the organization will assume you have the will and skill to deliver it. Most centrally, so too will your staff. What makes this expectation even more challenging is that they have grown up in an era when coaching in all its diverse manifestations is readily available to them as consumers. They may have used life-coaches, relationship coaches, prosperity coaches, fitness coaches or even parenting coaches in other areas of their lives, and they have absorbed from them a sense of the difference that focused attention can make.

The Millennials: are they really different?

If all this is becoming worrying, then there is a whole literature to increase your anxiety. A best-selling French book extols the virtues of workers shirking work as a rational response to its meaningless.[3] In this argument, since most of what office workers do is pointless and very few experience real success, workers should protect themselves by doing the minimum possible. This view of work is endorsed in the burgeoning world of blogging. The internet hums with accounts of disaffected employees. 'My life lost all meaning the day I joined', wrote one blogger, 'I create absolutely no value to society. I just help move data from one place to another'. Perhaps even more worrying from a corporate perspective, another blogger writes, 'I think one reason I stay here is because it is easy to be mediocre'.[4] While this view of work appeals to the cynic in us all, it denies the reality that if you have ever worked in a job that you perceive as pointless, it has a profound effect on self-esteem. Most people, while recognizing that ultimately there are more important things in life than work, still want to feel a sense of connection with what they do, and to believe that it matters. Their manager has a key role in creating that sense of connection and meaning, or in its absence.

Back in the 1980s Douglas Coupland wrote *Generation X*,[5] which highlighted that the generation coming after the baby-boomers of the post-World War 2 era, posed a challenge to organizations. They did not buy into the idea of organizational careers in terms of identifying with an institution, but did want success in terms of acquiring skills and experiences that would ensure their marketability. They have been labelled by Bruce Tulgan[6] as 'self-builders'. That does not mean that they want to do it all themselves, but that they value people they work with for the degree to which they can help them build their desired future. A manager is valued who can teach them, push them, believe in their abilities and provide opportunities. They seek evidence of the value of their own contribution and look for recognition, in order to confirm whether it is worth staying. So far, you may have been agreeing, because this describes you. You may well be a Generation Xer, born between 1963 and 1977, and have noticed that your own feelings about your working life have rested on such measures. You have worked well for a manager who offered support in your self-building and have even left a job because of a manager who did not.

All this is fine whilst you are the recipient of this attention, it looks different when you are in the provider role. If you are a Generation Xer you may well be managing those who have been labelled either Generation Y or Millennials. Generation Y's – those born after 1977 – have been described as 'Generation X on fast forward'.[7]

Add to expectations of challenge and responsibility that the challenge should have personal meaning; that the delegated responsibility should allow them to define how and where the work is delivered; and that their manager should create a fun environment, and it becomes frightening. Michel Syrett and Jean Lammiman, writing about Millennials from a UK perspective,[8] warn that they want to be inspired, but approach office life with a negative mindset that has to be won over; that Millennials believe their commitment has to be earned and sustained, that it does not come as part of their automatic offering and that they will walk away from an organization if there are no opportunities to show their individualism. Written in these bald terms it reads like a mantra for spoilt children. It may well evoke those feelings in you, as a Millennial requests a discussion about their career future or their personal development, just months after their arrival. The skill of the manager is to stand back and consider what might be the benefit in working with this perspective, and to determine what you need to offer in order to obtain those benefits.

Coaching as part of the psychological contract

To view coaching as an enabler to achieving what you need of a staff member, as well as an expectation they may have as an attention-hungry Millennial, it is helpful to recognize coaching's value within the psychological contract you have with staff. The psychological contract is a term first coined in the 1960s to describe the expectations that an organization and an employee have of each other, and that, if such expectations are met, provide a glue between the two. It came into focus in the 1990s[9] when the impact of global competition, the influence of Information Technology on how business could be done, economic conditions in the UK and changing patterns of employment made it apparent that the assumptions that individuals had of their employer in areas such as job security and career progression, and the assumptions that organizations had about staff, such as that they would trust the motives of the employer, value security and offer unconditional loyalty, were no longer accepted. The old 'deal' was being broken by both parties and a new one had to be constructed which worked with changes that were occurring both within businesses and within individuals.

The psychological contract that now operates for many staff, regardless of the economic cycle, is likely to include some of the features shown in Figure 1.1.

What is apparent in this 'deal' is that there is no expectation of a long-term relationship or long-term job security. The deal is conditional, but this does not mean that every employee constantly has their eye on the

Employee Offers	Employee Expects
• To work hard	• Reward commensurate with performance
• To show loyalty to their immediate work team	• Recognition for what they bring to the team
• To be flexible	
• To learn and develop	• Flexibility in how they are allowed to deliver work
• To deliver against the department's objectives	• Challenges that provide the sort of learning they value
• To be measured against delivery on their own objectives	• Feedback that recognizes contribution as well as feedback on underperformance
• To be stretched by taking on extra responsibilities	• To be given managerial support so that they can deliver

Figure 1.1   The psychological contract

exit door. Rather, they will stay for as long as the 'deal' is delivering from their perspective. From their side this means that central to their retention is attention from the person who is the most significant shaper of their perception of their 'deal' – their line manager. An organization has an identity or 'brand' that shapes why individuals are attracted to it but, once employed within it, the quality of their psychological contract is directly influenced by the degree to which their expectations are met by their manager.

What is new in this?

Everything I have written so far suggests that the case for coaching by managers is based on responding to the 'uppity demands' of an increasingly ego-centric workforce. That is not my case. Rather, I believe that what the writers on newly identified populations such as the Millennials have done is to re-package and re-label universal truths through allying them to visible changes in how work is done, or societal shifts. In doing so they suggest that it is the impact of technology that has brought about the increasing need for attention or an increase in time spent at work, and the growth of solo living that means people expect more of their relationship with their boss. In reality, people have always responded to attention as a means of enhancing their motivation and performance.

Rather than seeing coaching within work as a growth industry, born of a current fascination with having someone available to help deal with any aspect of your life, and legitimated by increased pressures within work, the real case for coaching staff is its centrality to employee motivation.

Early in their management development every manager is introduced to theories on human motivation. The work of Abraham Maslow[10] in defining a hierarchy of need, proposed that once a need has been met, an individual will seek to satisfy a need at the next level. In his hierarchy, once basic physiological needs are met, e.g. pay, warmth and shelter, an individual's attention will shift to their desire for security and order in their lives. Once an individual is certain that the environment provides those certainties then attention will focus on higher-order needs of affiliation, respect, status and the opportunity to act out their view of themselves within work. For talented marketable employees, the needs that they bring to work are of the higher order. They seek to be respected, and see managerial attention as a signal that they are valued. They feel respected when their views are listened to. They feel respected when mistakes they make are used to help them do it differently next time, rather than as an excuse for attacking their identity. If their identity with work is strong, then they will value being supported in becoming the person that they want to be, through seeing that their manager has an investment in supporting that process.

Similarly, another leading thinker on motivation, Frederick Herzberg,[11] in his work conducted in the 1950s and 1960s, found that motivators were the prime source of job satisfaction, and that the motivators that mattered to people were responsibility, growth and recognition for their achievement. The focus on salary, which is the attention of many employee discussions on motivation and frequently stated reason for job moves, disguises the reality that insufficient money demotivates, but money of itself is an inadequate motivator of job satisfaction. Human Resources (HR) has the means of preventing demotivation through its skill in matching reward systems to skill and performance. However, it is the manager's skill in providing individuals with a degree of responsibility appropriate to their abilities, in providing opportunities for growth in line with their desired learning and in giving recognition of the sort they value that makes the real difference.

How can a manager motivate?

The work on motivation suggests that managers have a key role. Much of the work on leadership points to the motivating power of the inspirational leader: the leader who has a clear vision and can articulate it with passion and a persuasive logic. However, experience tells us that, while inspiration can work in the moment of their presence, other people cannot motivate us in a way that is sustainable. Being told you need to lose weight, get fitter, be tidier, drink less, give up smoking or do more about the house, does not drive motivation to respond to those challenges. Any change that occurs happens when we find a motivation within us to address the issue. Wanting the approval of a new partner may drive weight loss in a way the words of a doctor never did. Getting fitter can happen when it is linked to supporting a charity that you care about, when paying membership for a gym never got you out the house. Handling more responsibility with enthusiasm does not come from being told it is a good thing but comes when that responsibility is attached to something that matters to you, whether that is learning, enhanced visibility, being able to lead others, being involved in something that is important to the business, the possibility of promotion or job security. The skill of a manager is not in providing motivation, but in understanding what motivates others and helping the individual to work with their motivators.

This is particularly important with your 'problem' people. Nigel Nicholson of the London Business School, puts the argument succinctly; 'You can't motivate difficult people, only they can. The manager's job is to create the conditions in which their inherent motivation – the natural commitment and drive that most people have – is freed and channelled toward achievable goals'.[12]

The manager does not need to find a sales angle that will persuade the individual to behave differently, e.g. 'Do I give a kick in the pants?' 'Should I try and appeal to their sense of loyalty to the team?'. Neither should they assume that their own motivators will work for the other person. The challenge is to unearth what the other's motivations are, and then to use them to lever the performance you need.

Using a martial arts analogy, victory in judo comes from finding the other person's locus of energy and then leveraging it to achieve your ends. Within work, if the employee is not doing what you need of them, instead of pushing solutions onto them, coaching is a powerful means of pulling solutions out of them.

At last, the link with coaching

So far, the chapter has been building the argument for managers coaching staff from a number of perspectives:

- a growing organizational expectation of managers
- a growing expectation of employees who have grown up in an era when coaching, in multiple manifestations, is permeating society
- a way of responding to an increasingly demanding and egocentric workforce
- a means of delivering the 'deal' that employees now expect
- a recognition that employees have always had motivations that, if better understood, can be used for organizational benefit

What has not been addressed is what is meant by coaching, and how applying coaching can help managers work with employees in ways that will help the individual deliver results, and not overwhelm the manager. Coaching is a means of using your daily interactions with staff in a more purposeful way. It does not mean your conversations will be carried out in a formal setting, or with hour-long slots. You recognize the interactions are more effective because you see an outcome from conversations, and your staff member knows they are different (even if they cannot articulate it) because they experience a qualitative difference. You and they may not even talk about the conversations as coaching conversations. They may see them as helpful 'chats', but you will know that you have applied structure and techniques in the managing of that conversation.

So what is coaching?

There are many definitions of coaching, but to strip things to their essentials, coaching is essentially 'two people engaged together in raising the awareness of one of them, and therefore their ability to act'.[13] Underpinning that simple definition, however, are a number of challenges:

- How able is the manager to engage the other person?
- How does the manager help the individual to gain awareness?
- How does the manager keep the focus on insight for action when the individual may be fascinated by awareness for its own sake or even the problem itself?
- How does the manager ensure that they are focusing on what is business relevant?

The remainder of this book will address these challenges, but clues as to what is required of the manager as coach are given in another definition of coaching used by The Work Foundation. They define coaching as 'helping someone see their situation clearly and calmly in order that they can make better decisions about what they do'. The requirement of managers in coaching staff is to be able to stand apart from the issue, so that they can help the other see the situation from different perspectives, with the aim of helping that person make a decision that is right for them and that motivates action.

These words are easy to write, but the reality of implementing them is challenging. It is difficult to sit outside a situation if that person's performance is creating problems for you. It is hard to accept a person's decision on what to do, if you can see that there are better decisions that you would make. Just as it is easy to see what friends should do in dealing with relationship or parenting problems when they can't.

It is because it is difficult that this book is written to offer you frameworks for dealing with the diversity of individual styles, motivations and ambitions of those who report to you. It is written not in order to make you a psychologist, but to make you more effective in your managerial role.

How much time?

Your concerns are likely to be around the time implications. How do you make coaching implementable when it is so often easier to send an email saying what you want of them, or to avoid giving feedback for risk of the reaction. Since so many of our actions within work are done in order to try and protect our time, what is the case for offering more of yourself to staff?

CASE STUDY

Kay was at the bottom of the management structure of a large food retailer, with responsibility for one section of the store. She had noticed that some produce was not selling and suspected it was the way it was displayed. She said nothing, however, because she assumed it was not her role, and that others would know better. One day, a regional manager visited the store and started to chat to her about her area. Feeling he had some interest, she asked him 'Do you think this layout works?'. Expecting him to share his far greater knowledge of retailing by telling her what to do, she was surprised when he replied, 'What do you think isn't working?'. She told him her perspective, in order that he would solve the problem, and was flattered when he responded, 'It sounds as though you understand what the problem is, what do you think we should change?'. Emboldened, she told him. To which he replied 'So, what is stopping you from doing it?'. 'I did not think I could', she responded. 'Who has told you not to use your initiative?', he questioned. To which the truthful response was 'No-one'.

Kay repeated this story to me many years after the conversation because it had had a profound effect on her, not only at the time, but in her subsequent management of staff. What she had learnt was not just that a manager can inspire confidence in the ability to act, but that a short interaction can have a big impact. She had never worked anywhere where managers had the time to sit down to coach, but she believed profoundly in the power of coaching for performance.

Although at the time Kay would not have recognized that she was receiving coaching, what she registered was:

- the manager had shown her the respect of listening to her
- he had challenged her assumptions
- he had encouraged her to identify a solution (which may not have been his solution to the problem)
- he had encouraged her to use her awareness as a motivation to act
- he had modelled an approach that she continued to use to great effect.

Contrast this with my recent experience as a late learner of keyboards. The teacher, considerably younger than myself, uses the lessons to bombard me with theory, which I am incapable of absorbing. He keeps me in a lesson for an hour when after thirty minutes my head is reeling. He ignores the book I bring, which includes songs that I enjoy and could imagine myself playing along to, and determines what I should be playing. He does not ask me how I learn best, tells me his approach, and then expresses surprise that I cannot move my fingers across the keyboard at speed. 'It is hard to imagine why someone can't do it, when you can yourself', he commented after watching one of my painful attempts.

Standing on the outside as a coach, I can see that he feels intimidated by being asked to teach a middle-aged woman when his average pupil is pre-teen. He feels that he will gain credibility with me by showing his theoretical credentials and displaying that his approach is different from previous teachers who have struggled to get my two hands moving together with any fluidity. What is missing from this is any awareness of me, my feelings at attempting to learn a new skill, my goals and motivations. What I am learning are my own inadequacies. As a provider of a service, this works to his financial advantage, in that he shows me that I need considerable teaching help, but he fails to engender any enthusiasm to rush home and practise.

Transfer this back into the workplace, and you can see the parallels:

- the manager who, on being brought a work issue, uses it as an opportunity to display their superior knowledge
- the manager who fails to recognize that individuals have anxieties and concerns, as distinct from skills deficits, in taking on new challenges

- the manager who does not take the time to discover an individual's preferred way of approaching a task, and assumes it is their way
- the manager who leaves you feeling even less adequate at the end of an interaction, with the result that you either go away and don't ask again, or that your confidence about delivering is reduced, leading you to want more and more input on what you should be doing.

Amongst managers there are many well-meaning instructors, who give of their time without gaining a performance pay off.

A Manager Coach gives of just enough time to ensure that the person is able to act. The four questions that need to be asked every time an employee seeks help are these:

F – How can I ensure this conversation is focused and has purpose?
A – Is this conversation moving towards their ability to take action?
S – Is this conversation helping the other person to find a solution, rather than holding onto the problem?
T – Is this conversation timely and time effective?

Working within the FAST framework, a coaching conversation can take minutes. Consider Kay's conversation.

F – It focused absolutely on Kay's concerns about her part of the store with the purpose of equipping her to take initiative.
A – The manager assumed that the aim was to enable Kay to take action, rather than to talk about the problems of layout.
S – He pulled the solution out from her, rather than pushing his solution.
T – The conversation was clearly timely, and it took no longer than it needed to take.

Good Manager Coaches are FAST. The rest of this book is about helping you become the best FAST coach that you can be. It will provide you with the STARTED framework for managing conversations, with tools that you can use, and case studies – case studies that relate to the issues typically brought to managers, when they are up against deadlines, about to go to an important meeting, facing a difficult conversation with their own boss, or about to leave the office for the weekend.

You already know a great deal that is helpful to coaching staff. The purpose of this book is to help you recognize what you know, and help you address blind spots. An added bonus is that by modelling this approach with your direct reports, you will equip them to deal with *their* reports, modelling the behaviours you have used with them.

Summary

- This chapter has laid out the ground as to why coaching is more than just a 'flavour of the month' management skill, but a valuable approach to motivating staff and thereby enabling them to meet your needs and their own needs.
- Coaching has been identified as 'two people engaged together in raising the awareness of one of them, and there͓ ͓their ability to act'. It is the focus on awareness for action that is͓ ͓ral to keeping both manager and staff member on target, and not͓ ͓ing into areas of discussion that either lead to insight without ac͓ ͓ or to levels of disclosure that the manager is unable to deal with.

The underpinning of all that follo͓ ͓this book is that in order for coaching to be used within a manageme͓ ͓ll set, rather than becoming the focus of a manager's role, it needs ͓ FAST.

References

1. Gladwell, M. (2͓ ͓ *The Tipping Point: How Little Things Can Make A Big Differenc͓* ͓acus.
2. CIPD (2004)͓ *ning and Development 2004: Survey Report.* CIPD.
3. Maier, C. (?͓ ͓) *Hello Laziness! Why Hard Work Doesn't Pay.* Orion.
4. Stern, S. (2005) Bad days at the office. *Financial Times Magazine*, 11 June, 36–37.
5. Coupland, D. (1991) *Generation X: Tales for an Accelerated Culture.* St Martin's Griffin.
6. Tulgan, B. (1997) *The Manager's Pocket Guide Book to Generation X.* HRD Press.
7. Tulgan, B. (2001) *Managing Generation Y.* HRD Press.
8. Syrett, M. and Lammiman, J. (2003) Catch them if you can. *Director Magazine*, October, 70–76.
9. Herriot, P. and Pemberton, C. (1995) *New Deals: The Revolution in Managerial Careers.* John Wiley and Sons.

10. Maslow, A. (1970) *Motivation and Personality.* Harper and Row.
11. Herzberg, F. (2003) One more time: how do you motivate employees? *Harvard Business Review,* January, 87–96.
12. Nicholson, N. (2003) How to motivate problem people. *Harvard Business Review,* January, 56–75.
13. Definition of John Leary Joyce, CEO of Academy of Executive Coaching.

2

The coach in you

The greatest challenge to any thinker is stating the problem in a way that will allow a solution.

Bertrand Russell

We will return to FAST in future chapters. For this chapter, the focus is on you – because beyond any technique that coaching can offer, the most powerful tool you bring to a coaching conversation is yourself.

You already hold within you many of the skills required in coaching. You use them every day of your life and you probably don't even consider them valuable.

In order to be capable of coaching staff within an organization you need:

- to believe that people are capable of change
- to believe that you make a difference to how people approach their work
- to believe that coaching is not a special skill that sits apart from every-day interactions.

My earliest work role was in helping disabled school leavers move beyond education and into work. As part of my development I was sent on a programme to help develop my skills in enabling disabled teenagers to talk about their hopes, fears and anxieties in moving from the protected environment of residential schooling to a judgemental world where their disabilities marked them out as different and disadvantaged. As the course leader outlined the skills that were about to be taught, the person sitting next to me whispered, 'I don't know why I am here, the person who does all this stuff at our school is the cleaner'. Within that school the children recognized that the person who could most easily allow them to be themselves and to talk about whatever was worrying them, was the person who the school would have assessed as being least trained for the role. In reality, she provided a sanctuary within her cleaning cupboard where adolescents knew they would be taken seriously, listened to and allowed to be honest. She had no power to fix things for them, she had no solutions to issues that were complex, but pupils left that cupboard feeling helped.

The cleaning cupboard is a good analogy for coaching, because coaching is about creating a place of safety whilst surrounded by the reality of work. Space where people can find a way through the things that are making life difficult for them, before stepping back out of the cupboard into the maelstrom of daily life, better equipped to deal with it.

When students came to that cupboard they did not come because of her formal qualifications and training, they came because they innately recognized that she had the skills to help them.

We know that we choose to talk with some people rather than others when we are feeling anxious about the pressures of work. There is a distinction, however, between identifying people who will listen to us, and identifying those who will listen in order to try and help us deal with the difficulty. Unearthing what contributes to a conversation being helpful rather than simply offering an opportunity to dump emotions and dissatisfactions is important if the conversations are to be more than pressure-easing chats. Some clues have been provided by work done by the National Institute for Careers Education and Counselling (NICEC).[1] They asked people in both the public and private sectors:

- when they had had a helpful conversation
- what happened in the conversation
- what was different for them as a consequence.

Their findings showed that:

- helpful conversations were far more likely to take place in informal situations than at formal appointments. Never underestimate the power of the chat in the cleaning cupboard or the unplanned conversation on a car journey
- a one-off conversation is often all that is needed or sought. A focused conversation that leads to change is success for both sides. It is ineffectual conversations that lead to repeat performances
- the helpful outcomes of the conversations were more likely to be about the individual gaining an insight, than the helper fixing something or taking responsibility for them. It was being able to see things differently that led the seeker of help to do something different as a result of the other's input
- good conversations can take place anytime and anywhere. It is getting the timing right for the individual that is key.

Helpful conversations, because they are delivered with focused attention and a laser eye on outcome, do not bring the person back again and again.

Some years ago research showed that patients expected seven minutes attention from their GP. Nowhere was this figure written down, but an internal clock interacting with a sense of self-worth told patients that if they got less than seven minutes they were short-changed, and they kept coming back. This created a vicious circle where patients felt they were not being heard so they came back, which in turn increased the pressure on doctors who shortened their contact time with each patient, which in turn increased the patients' need to come back for a top up of time.

This may explain why current British Medical Association guidelines now recommend a consultation period of no less than seven minutes. Transferred to organizations, this means: give people the quality of attention they need at the time they need it and they don't come back again and again. Give people time while your attention is elsewhere, or attention at the wrong time, and the benefits are lost. It is being available in the right way at the right time that enables people to use your time and skills appropriately. This is hard to trust when you are under pressure and overworked, but the most powerful way in which you can help staff is to be available to them at their time of need.

This is where coaches internal to the organization have an enormous advantage over any external coach. An external provider comes in, on average, monthly. They are unlikely to be present when the most significant things are happening to their client. They are rarely around in the minutes following a difficult meeting, a performance management discussion that went badly, the announcement of business results that could result in redundancies, a client presentation that fell apart – moments when a coaching input could have a powerful impact. Externals lack the power of timeliness, of being there at exactly the right moment. Because of this, situations are reconstructed weeks after the event with all the inevitable distortions that come with time and the retelling of a story. The closer you can be to the moment, the more truthful in its content and its emotion will be the telling.

As an internal you have the advantage of flexibility. You meet at coffee machines, hang around at the end of meetings, share a drink in a bar at the end of the day. All of this is denied external coaches, who are brought into formal space at a pre-arranged time. Their rules of behaviour have been influenced by the rules of therapy: sessions of a defined length, set times for meetings, minimal contact between sessions, meetings in professional space set apart from the working space, relationships that are contractually defined. None of this is true for internals. Whilst this can create difficulties in separating out the role of performance manager from the role of performance coach, it also means you are not hidebound by conventions.

When as an external coach I suggested to a client who was visibly exhausted by a day of confrontational meetings that we move to a café so he could step away from an environment that was draining him and have a cigarette whilst we work, I felt unsure if I had contravened some professional ground rule. When a manager suggests to a staff member that they get away from the office to give them the chance to speak more easily about what is troubling them, the employee feels gratitude that their need for some neutral space has been recognized, and you are halfway to the conversation being useful.

Yin and yang: support and challenge

The NICEC study highlighted more than the value of informality and timeliness in helping staff. It also focused on what managers actually do that enables the conversations to be helpful. They highlighted two key elements:

SUPPORT and CHALLENGE

Support did not mean that they said:

- Of course you couldn't help messing up that video-conference yesterday. It's not your fault you got the time wrong.
- It must be awful having to deal with . . .
- Don't worry, I will fix it for you.
- I'll have a word in her ear and tell her not to give you a hard time.
- It's not fair the way your team don't appreciate you.

It meant instead that they:

- *Listened* closely for the content and the meaning of that content to the individual

   I can tell from your face that you are upset at having done less than your best at that video-conference yesterday.

■ *Showed Genuine Interest* in the issue as it impacted on the other person whilst keeping the context in mind.

> *I would be happy to help you find a way of dealing with those customers more effectively because your relationship with them is not doing your confidence, or your sales figures, any good right now.*

■ *Were Positive.* They looked for what could be built on, rather than focusing only on the difficulty.

> *Just because it went wrong this time doesn't mean that all your reports miss the mark. I have seen many others that have been fine. I would like us to find a way of getting your work back on track through identifying where the report was weak, and recognizing what was good, so that you can take back responsibility for finishing off the work.*

■ *Encouraged Openness* to the degree that was relevant to the issue being discussed. They did not encourage openness for its own sake, so that the individual felt that they had revealed too much about themselves.

> *If you can be honest enough to tell me what you find difficult about my approach, then we can try and work out ways of managing our relationship difficulty. If you don't tell me I will fill in the space, and I will probably be wrong.*

Similarly, when NICEC spoke of Challenge they did not mean:

■ Why the hell did you say that in front of the CEO?
■ That's a stupid idea, it would never work.
■ You could do it your way or you could do it mine. Guess which one is more career progressive?
■ Is that really the best you can do?

Instead they meant that skilled helpers:

■ *Challenged constructively.* They looked for what could be built on, ensuring that whatever they offered was done in order to move things forward rather than to crush the other person.

> *I can see why you think the way you do about how to grow the customer base, but I think you are overlooking some key elements. Let me throw in another perspective and see where it takes your thinking?*

What I think is workable in your solution is this ... What I would like you to think some more about is this ...

■ *Gave Honest Feedback.* They were willing to take the risk of fracturing the rapport they had built up with the other person, through saying what they thought would be helpful in bringing about a shift.

It would be easy for me to say don't worry about the meeting today, those people are not very senior. But, I think it would be more helpful to you to give you some feedback on the impact on me of what I saw you do today.

I know you are ambitious for promotion, and have great abilities, but if you are to achieve what you want for yourself you need to show more than talent and drive. What could derail you is the perception others have of you, the perception you saw reflected in the 360 degree feedback, that you are only interested in your own contribution and ignore those of others.

I was disappointed with the work you have done on this project. I could quietly shift you to another piece of work, but I know you want to succeed with this, so I am going to give you some feedback, so that you have the opportunity to put it right.

In this view of Support and Challenge:

■ *Support* is not about rescuing others or finding excuses, it is about signalling that you are willing to help them work out how they can do it better for themselves.
■ *Challenge* is not about showing that you are their manager because you think and do better than they are capable of. It is about signalling that, because you are outside of their situation, you look at it through a different lens to the one they hold, and that you are going to use that lens to help them see more options in how they deal with the difficulty.

Thought and action

Challenge and Support are invaluable but they are even more powerful when they are allied to Thought and Action.

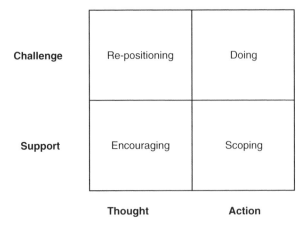

	Thought	Action
Challenge	Re-positioning	Doing
Support	Encouraging	Scoping

Figure 2.1 Challenge, support, thought and action

- *Challenge for Thought* means asking questions that force the other person to take another look at their own analysis.
- *Support for Thought* means creating the climate in which the other person can speak freely, bringing into the open thoughts they may not previously have expressed.
- *Challenge for Action* means keeping in focus the need to turn talk into solutions, and solutions into actions.
- *Support for Action* means ensuring that the size of the action is commensurate with their abilities and confidence.

Every person who comes to you needs support and challenge, but they need it in different amounts depending on their individual style, and they need it in different amounts each time you talk.

Getting the balance wrong

Alison was a secretary in the not-for-profit sector. She had worked there for several years after a chequered work history where she reported that she had always been let down by the person she worked for. This time she had struck lucky. She had been working for a boss whom she clearly worshipped because 'he understood her'. What this meant in practice was that he gave her large amounts of supportive affirmation and chose to ignore the behaviours she used on others, which were highly critical and authoritarian. In return for his turning a blind eye, she was as protective as a lioness in controlling access to him and making his life easy. Her one complaint was that she could not understand why other younger staff were being appointed to junior management roles when she had never been asked to apply. Her boss never explained, he simply affirmed her indispensability to him. He had taken the decision not to explain because she became aggressive at any hint of criticism. He assumed that encouragement through support for thought was the only zone she could operate from.

While Alison did have high support needs, she also needed to be challenged through feedback if she was to be capable of moving outside of the particular dynamic that she and her boss had created. Inevitably, her boss did leave, and when he did she acted as though she had been abandoned. Now there was no one whose support she could count on, and without having had the opportunity to develop beyond her role, she read it as another example of being let down.

Getting the balance right

Jim was a highly analytical senior manager in an organization that depended on the calibre of its intellect. He could be arrogant and spoke with pride of his arrogance, which he interpreted as intellectual superiority. His behaviour was tolerated because it was understood that he could find solutions to problems where others had failed. His bosses had, in response, taken a 'hands off' approach to him. His nemesis came in the form of a new boss who was strong on 'hands on', and who would not accept that Jim had all the answers and did not need anyone else's input. He began to shift work around, signalling that he would rather have less able direct reports who he could manage than a difficult genius. He was implicitly challenging Jim through his actions. Jim was both enraged at his boss's actions, and knocked sideways in his confidence. His enabling challenge came not from his boss but from his secretary. She pointed out that if he did not find a way of dealing with the new Director he was in danger of having his role totally taken from under his feet. 'You have to find a way of making it OK with him, and stop waiting for him to make it OK for you'. Startled by this provocation from someone who had always been 100 per cent supportive, he took action. Shortly after, he took his boss out for a drink and said that he wanted to improve their working relationship, but it was hard for him being micro-managed. In return, his boss owned that it was hard for him to manage someone whose intellect outstripped his own and who, from his perspective, belittled him.

The meeting did not end in a warm embrace after cathartic disclosure, but it was the start of a shift in their relationship. Without the challenge to Jim's thinking by his secretary, the possibility of change would not have been available.

The four elements of conversations for change

Every helping conversation needs four elements:

1. *Support for Thought.* An environment in which the other person is encouraged to say what they think and feel without fearing consequences and with the trust that the manager wants them to share their thoughts and feelings as a means for resolving the difficulty.
2. *Challenge for Thought.* A second voice that asks questions the individual does not ask themselves, not in order to show cleverness but in order to widen the lens through which the other person accesses the information on which they base their decisions.
3. *Challenge for Action.* People are often comfortable analysing a problem to death and interpret understanding as a substitute for action. For a manager, coaching only to aid understanding is a luxury. Coaching is unjustifiable unless it can be allied to action. The challenge for action in any coaching conversation is to enable the other person to 'do one thing differently' as a result of their time with you.
4. *Support for Action.* Once action is defined, the skill of the Manager Coach is in offering the support that will make it possible. Support means more than words of encouragement: the basis of the 'where there is the will there is the skill' school of coaching. Support means helping to scope the size of the action so that there is a high chance of success, and confronting the reality of how much or little confidence the other person has for action once they walk away from the conversation. 'Of course you can do it', is less useful than asking 'How confident do you feel that you can do what you have committed to, and what will increase your confidence in taking action?'.

Remove any of the four elements and the likelihood of an effective outcome is reduced:

- *Support for Thought without Challenge for Action* results in enjoyable conversations with no clear outcome.

- *Challenge for Action without Support for Thought* results in the other person feeling bulldozed into doing something without fully understanding or committing.
- *Challenge for Thought without Support for Thought* leads to intellectual sparring for its own sake, disconnected from the other person's purpose and context.
- *Support for Thought without Challenge for Thought* allows the individual to present their perception of the world as though it represents total reality, and denies them the opportunity to reframe their thinking and therefore the options available to them.
- *Challenge for Action without Support for Action* results in overambitious goals with little likelihood for success.
- *Support for Action without Challenge for Action* can lead to the manager becoming the motivator and cheerleader, without the individual taking responsibility for stretching themselves.

Every coaching conversation is a dance between Support and Challenge, Thought and Action. The skill of the coach is in being able to judge which position is most useful at any point in time.

In reality each of us has developed a preferred mix of the four as our instinctive position when dealing with others who seek our help.

When a manager responds to a request for help by saying:

- 'Just get out there and do something.'
- 'Get it in perspective.'
- 'Tell me what's worrying you and I will see what I can do.'
- 'Don't get emotional about this.'
- 'Of course you can deal with it.'
- 'You had better sort it all, else there will be trouble.'
- 'Tell me what is making this difficult for you, two heads are usually better than one?'

they are signalling the model that they have developed as their means of dealing with the demands placed on them. Within that model there will be space that has been allocated for support and a space that has been allocated for challenge; space for thought and space for action. The relative sizes of those zones will have been shaped by their life experience, and instinctively they will use it as their basis for helping others.

Understanding your model

Each of us has a way of approaching an invitation to help another based on what our lives have taught us. Because they are based on messages that we have acted on and that have worked for us, we trust them. The extension of this is that we assume they will work for others. This may not be true.

When we offer to coach another person it is important to ask ourselves what we are bringing to the process. Of course, you are explicitly bringing a range of work experience that is greater than the person who has sought you out. However, what you and they may fail to recognize is the implicit model that will shape how you react to them.

To understand your model ask yourself these questions:

- Based on your experience of being brought up in your family, what were the messages that have stuck with you from childhood? These may be direct messages from your parents, e.g. 'Only hard work gets rewarded', 'It's the winning that counts'. 'It is important to put others before yourself'. Or they may be messages that you gave yourself as a result of being part of your family, e.g. 'It is important to succeed in order that I don't have the sort of life that my parents have had', 'Being successful is not worth having if it means you don't have time for living'.

- What have been your most difficult life experiences, and what have you taken from them? For example, 'You can't trust other people, when the chips are down', 'When the going gets tough it is having a helping hand that gets you through', 'Never give up – something good always comes out of something bad', 'Just do something, anything which stops you focusing on the bad stuff', 'There's no point just taking action, you have to live with the difficult for as long as it takes.'

- Who are the people who have most influenced you at work and what did they teach you? For example, 'Always focus on the task and don't allow anyone or anything to deflect you', 'It is important to push people beyond their comfort level', 'Focus on understanding the other person and you will get the result you want', 'Make sure you only do the things which will get the attention of your bosses'.

The answers to these questions will influence where you sit most comfortably on those two axes of Support and Challenge.

CASE STUDY

Graham was a board member of a medium-sized private company. He had poor relations with his board colleagues because they saw him as a 'know it all' who leapt in to provide answers to their problems within seconds of them opening their mouths. In his mind he was saving them time, because his thought processes were rapid and often his answers were right – even if it took them a while to get round to recognizing it. He could not understand why they got upset when he was offering a time-efficient solution. When pushed, he recognized that his solutions usually evoked visual signs of resistance in his colleagues, but he chose to block those out. He was a man who valued himself for his ability to Challenge for Thought and to Challenge for Action.

Graham's model, which ignored the need to offer space for other people to think things through or to let them scope their own solution, were based on a powerful personal model:

- Growing up in a highly intellectual family where you gained attention for the power of your thinking, and where meal times were a competitive battlefield.
- Working for bosses who were highly authoritarian, demanding and critical.
- The early death of a parent that was dealt with through not talking about the event or the emotional impact on him as young child, but by taking control of the practical aspects.

All of these messages were brought into the workplace and applied rigorously. A direct report who came asking for help with a piece of work would be subjected to an interrogation in order to sharpen up their analytical skills. Staff bruised by encounters when they had asked for feedback face to face quickly learnt to deal with him by email. Fellow directors would keep him in the dark about issues in order to minimize his input.

What is lost in this account is that Graham was not a terrible human being. In person he was fun and charming, and he was absolutely committed to the organization. His limitations were a life model that only allowed for Challenge as the basis for helping others to deliver more.

When he recognized that what he would have welcomed in his early years, i.e. Support, was exactly what his colleagues and direct reports

> wanted from him, he began to approach his encounters with them differently.

Each of us is skewed in a different way in how we approach the invitation to help another person. Some of us are skewed towards Support for Thought in ways that make people feel comfortable, but that can also allow them to avoid taking responsibility for action. Others are skewed towards offering Support for Action when we could make a real difference through challenging the other person to aim higher. We may enjoy the dance of challenging thought without considering how to move it into action.

The challenge for any manager who is asked to coach is to recognize their own preference and then to challenge themselves to develop to more fully occupy the four positions of coaching influence.

Summary

In this chapter we have focused on:

- The importance of creating cupboard space for your direct reports to bring their performance issues.
- The value of timeliness as a powerful agent in change.
- The need in every coaching conversation for the elements of Support and Challenge balanced with Thought and Action.
- The preferences that each of us bring to our coaching conversations, based on the learning from which we have taken our key life experiences.
- The importance of widening our range if we are to help others.

Reference

1. Hirsh, W., Jackson, C. and Kidd, J. (2001) *Straight Talking*. NICEC.

3

Before you assess others, assess yourself

Honesty is the first chapter in the book of wisdom.
Thomas Jefferson

I ran a programme to help managers coach their staff. Like most managers they were highly pragmatic in their approach. Energy dropped every time a piece of theory was introduced and rose immediately they had the chance to talk with each other about real life issues that were impacting on them. Asked to coach each other to find a way forward, the conversations followed a predictable path:

John would start telling Tim the details of his work issue, which usually concerned someone they both knew.

Tim would ask John a few questions and, within a minute or less, would be offering his views on that individual and his solution to the matter.

Sometimes John showed some resistance to Tim's solution, which undermined Tim's instant answer, but then acted as a spur for Tim to work harder to come up with a solution. With every minute that passed John talked less and less while Tim talked more and more, generously offering his wisdom for John's benefit. Alternately, if John was an amiable sort, and if Tim was more senior, he would readily accept Tim's ideas and they would quickly divert the conversation onto other matters.

Both would report back after the exercise that they had enjoyed talking with each other, and John would express his appreciation of Tim's efforts.

Follow up when the group reconvened a month later would show that John had not implemented Tim's solution. Neither seemed bothered by this outcome, since the act of getting to know each other better had been its own reward. Tim did not take offence at his solution not being accepted because it had occurred off line. Had he spent that amount of time talking with John back at work, and John had been a direct report, he would have expressed irritation at the wasted effort and time he had given on John's behalf, when he was already busy.

This highlights the first paradoxical rule of helping others

The harder you are working for them, the less likely they are to commit to your solution.

This seems counter-intuitive. Surely, they want you to make life easier for them by shortcutting their anxiety, and sharing your wisdom. Strangely, they don't. Look at the dance that is played out in work every day.

One person asks another for help. The other person, recognizing that the first is struggling, decides to help through offering advice, i.e. this is what I would do if I were you. The advice is quickly forgotten and nothing changes. Or think of those conversations with friends when you have poured out the failings of a partner, only to feel affronted if they tell you to ditch them and get on with your life. You wanted to be listened to, you did not want them to solve the problem.

When people try to produce solutions for the problems of others, the unrecognized subtext is that we can never experience the problem in the way that they do. We are each a unique tapestry, constructed of how we see the world around us, how we respond to situations, what we believe we can do and not do, our abilities, our motivations and our values. When we look to help others, we help best when we recognize what we instinctively bring of ourselves to the discussion, and then look to find ways of those things not getting in the way. By clearing ourselves out of the picture we can keep the searchlight on helping the other person move forward.

That is why the whole of this chapter is about YOU. Once you know what you bring, you can both recognize what will come easier to you, and what you will find more difficult. It will help you recognize why it is easier to work with some staff than others, and to stop your own style getting in the way of the style of a person who is very different from you.

CASE STUDY

Wendy was a Financial Controller in a successful start up. The business had grown rapidly, and she reported to a Financial Director who had been in from the beginning. He valued Wendy and was ambitious for her to move into the FD role when the time came for him to move on. He wanted Wendy to prepare herself for the role, and had regular discussions with her about how she needed to develop in order to broaden her experience. In particular he encouraged her to gain more visibility with Board members. Wendy loved what she did but she was clear that she did not want to be the number one. She hated visibility, and she did not want the accountability that being number one brought. Because she knew this was incomprehensible to her boss, she became evasive whenever the subject of her career was raised. She did not want to disappoint him by not being the person that he thought she was.

Wendy's story highlights *the second paradoxical rule of coaching*

They may value and respect you but that doesn't mean that they want their success to be like your success.

Understanding what the other person means by success is a compass point to recognizing what help they would really value.

This lesson was also not understood by Anthony, a Marketing Director working for a high-street retailer. Hearing I was running a career management programme that several of his direct reports had asked to attend, he rang me in an apoplectic state. 'Why?', he wanted to know 'should he spend company money on their attending a course when it was obvious what they needed to do to get on'. They just needed to talk to him and he would explain how he had done it. Missing from his model of helping was any sense that they might not want what he wanted.

Ask yourself the question, how will you know when you are successful, and you might answer:

- When I can buy a Ferrari/a vineyard in Burgundy/Armani suit/painting by . . .
- When I can retire early
- When I am a recognized authority
- When I have a balanced life
- When I have a job title with Director in it, and can fly first class
- When I am sought out by others because of my expertise
- When I feel I am using all the skills I most value
- When I am working in an organization whose values I share
- When I am invited to contribute to the most important projects my organization is involved in.

What would it be for you? Whatever you reply will reveal your own model of success. It is likely to fall under one of three headings.

1. *Tangible and Measurable.* Those things that you can see and touch and that others can recognize. It could be the car model, the job title, the office size or the size of the bonus, but it is important to you as a reflection of what you have achieved.
2. *Intangible but Visible.* Being invited to speak at company conferences; being included in key meetings because of your expertise; being used as a sounding board by managers who may be senior to you but recognize your particular skills. None of this may translate into salary, but when you receive these rewards it makes you feel good about what you do.
3. *Intangible and Out of Sight.* Success here could be linked to being associated with an organization you have always admired; being able to have a life at work that reflects who you are as a person; being able to create a whole life in which work is an integrated part but not the most important part.

In Wendy's case it is clear that her boss held a model based around tangibility, whereas for Wendy it was the intangible and visible that made her feel good about her working life. For Anthony, tangibility was the only model he could conceive of. If someone had presented their model of success as being based on internal factors such as continually challenging oneself, he would have dismissed it as a substitute for the 'real thing'.

Widen the issue out from career success to consider what success in a given task would look like, and the same issue arises. A team member may say they are concerned about giving a presentation at a large event, but what level of success are they looking for?

- To be able to overcome their deep-seated fear of talking to a group?
- To use a PowerPoint presentation creatively?
- To be able to talk fluently without notes?
- To raise key issues that they want to be looked at strategically?
- To leave a positive impression on the CEO?
- To do better than last time when they dropped their notes, left out half the speech and walked backwards off the stage?

Until you know what the other person means by success you risk offering help that they may mouth gratitude for, but that leads to no action. The closer you can match with their success model, the greater will be the impact of your input.

Which leads to the *third paradoxical rule of coaching:*

Goals are outputs not the starting point.

It is usual in coaching books to talk about the importance of goal setting. Define the goal at the start and the rest will follow. Decide you want to be promoted in a year and a clear path of action will emerge. State you want to be a better communicator and a development plan will follow. This pre-supposes that the person is clear about their goal at the start, which often they are not (a theme we will return to in Chapter 9). Often, all they know is that they are dissatisfied with something; whether that is their job, the way they are approaching their work or their relationships with key people. Meaningful goals, i.e. ones the individual really connects with so that they are committed to action, emerge from skilful conversations, and often late in those conversations.

What the coachee does know, even if they are unarticulated, are their values. Their values shape what they believe is possible for themselves, what they are willing to do and how they approach it. Just as the coach knows, even if unarticulated, their own values. Therefore, it makes sense as a coach to understand your own values in order that you can stop them getting in the way of the other person.

Values fall into the intangible but visible category. We can't see them but they are made visible in action. When someone turns down a promotion because it would involve uprooting their family, they are signalling a value. When a colleague claims credit for a piece of work, when in reality a junior member of staff did all the work, they reveal a value. When someone says they feel guilty about making a staff member redundant they reveal a value. When a colleague says that adopting a policy of each year sacking the bottom 10 per cent is the only way to keep people performing, they reveal a value. When you keep your office door open so that you are accessible you reveal a value, just as when you keep it closed in order to keep focused on what has to be delivered you reveal another.

If your values are not to get in the way of another person's thinking, it is important to understand what you bring. By understanding your own, you will then be more sensitized to recognizing the other person's.

Recognizing your own values

Some of your values have already been revealed in the previous chapter. In answering questions about what you have taken from your early life influences, from difficult life experiences and from key people in your career, you have started to unearth the values that shape how you focus your energy when you are having a coaching conversation. Look again at your answers and see if those values are now even clearer to you.

Another way of identifying your values is to consider the choices you make when you have to decide between conflicting choices.

Imagine you are going to an auction. At that auction is available a whole range of offerings and you can bid. Each item in the auction is implicitly signalling a value. You have available to you a sum of money equivalent to your age times 100. This currency is important because it assumes that the importance of recognizing and committing to our values increases with age.

On offer at the auction are the following items:

- the money to buy the . . . of your dreams (you fill in the gap)
- the guarantee of making a real difference through work
- fame for being . . . (you fill in the gap)
- a happy family life (however you construe family)
- good health into old age
- the knowledge that you will never be without work
- a contribution to wider society
- the opportunity to do something that will live on after you
- a sense of connection with your spirituality (however you construe spirit)
- the chance to do something you never thought you could do and succeeding
- recognition for your expertise in . . . (you fill in the gap)
- sporting success
- the chance to take a risk in your life through . . . (you fill in the gap)
- the opportunity to establish your own enterprise
- freedom from the constraints of an organization
- to use your skills to help others
- to head up an organization
- to advance the knowledge base within your area
- to do . . . (you fill in the gap) better than your peers
- to have a balanced life.

Which of those twenty items would you bid for, and how much would you be willing to risk on each item?

In a real auction you would almost certainly be outbid on certain of the items, so you could not take them home. In this auction, whatever you have bid for is already there within you, so the amount you were willing to risk is an indicator of how important it is for you.

Look at the items you have identified and ask yourself what that value says to you and how it translates into work. Look beyond the literal item and consider what it signals to you.

If you have bid for the house/car/yacht of your dreams then you may be carrying a value that says 'it is important that my success is signalled to others' or 'I only feel I am successful when I see what it buys', or 'It is only worth doing if it is financially rewarded'. Only you will know what the value says.

Whatever it says will translate into actions at work. In the process of translation it may lead you to do whatever is necessary in order to get the highest financial reward and to be judgemental of those who will not do the same. It may lead you to use a carrot and stick approach with staff in the belief that the promise of reward will motivate performance.

If you have bid for the knowledge that you will never be without work, the value that drives it may be shaped by a belief that 'Without work I have no identity' or 'It is important to always provide' or even 'Security is important as a sign of being an adult'. In work translation this may mean you are questioning of staff who are talented but show no intention of wanting to stay for the long haul, or that you only point out the risks when a colleague is looking to make a role change and asks your advice.

Equally important is how much you were willing to bid for each value. If you put all your money on one item, you can be sure it is a driving force in how you approach your work. If you bid for a number of them, then what is the hierarchy of importance for you?

We cannot help but translate our values into work. This is valid as a guide to helping us decide what we will be comfortable and less comfortable doing. It is less than helpful when we are looking to help another person think through their own issues and we impose our own values. We need instead to help them recognize their own values as a guide to them making the best decision for themselves.

You will have realized through managing staff that one of the reasons you gel with some of your direct reports better than others is because of the values match. Anthony, our Marketing Director, will unconsciously have identified those direct reports whose values best match with his own, and will happily share his advice because it will meet with a warm response. He will also have recognized those who do not share his values and have dismissed them as 'lacking what it takes'.

When managers coach they risk doing the same. When there is a deep feeling of comfort between the coach and the other it is usually because of matching. We match with those whose life experiences mirror our own, whose family and educational backgrounds are similar to ours, where outside interests are shared – but we also match or mismatch on the basis of values.

If you are going to stop your values getting in the way of helping another then it is important to bring them into awareness so that they do not unconsciously control your conversations.

Summarize for yourself

What I would bid for in a values auction	Its meaning for me	Its translation into my work	The risk of applying it in coaching another

Figure 3.1   Values assessment

Summary

In this chapter, the focus has been on how the manager can put themselves in the way of helping another through imposing their own models.

- You hold a model of success based on what you have experienced and the lessons you have taken from them. Everyone you coach will have done the same.
- Equally you carry a set of values that shapes the decisions you make throughout your working day, as does the other person.
- Neither are zero-sum games. Allowing another person's models does not undermine yours. Rather, when you help another person to understand their models they value you the more.
- The values and success exercises are tools you can use when looking to help another person understand what drives them.

We have also identified that the rules of coaching are paradoxical:

- The harder you are working for another person, the less likely they are to commit to your solution. Whereas when you are working with them, commitment will follow.
- They may value and respect you but that doesn't mean that they want their success to be like your success. Whereas when you help them to recognize what they need to be successful, their valuing of you will increase.
- Goals are outputs, not the starting point. Goals are enormously important, but good goals emerge from the process rather than being the driver of it.

4

Getting STARTED

Focus 90% of your time on solutions and only 10% on problems.

Anthony D'Angelo

Having built the case for coaching and encouraged you to consider what you bring to the conversation, which will influence how you approach helping others, it's time to define the approach to coaching that will shape the rest of this book. This will give you tools to effectively manage conversations to meaningful outcomes.

The approach is called Solution Focused. It is drawn from what has been learnt in a number of therapeutic disciplines where the helpers are looking to effect change quickly,[1–3] and the principles it uses are directly relevant to working in organizational settings. In writing the word 'therapy', it is important to state clearly that nothing that follows is about making you a therapist. There are key differences between coaching and therapy.

Is coaching therapy?

One way of separating the two is to understand that therapy is appropriate where a person is experiencing a difficulty that is significantly impacting on their own lives (and others), to the degree that the best way of helping them to resolve it is to give forensic attention to the problem. It is a telescopic process that involves looking at the past as the means of building understanding. From understanding, psycho-analytic therapies argue, change becomes possible.

Coaching, in contrast, is about working with people who are fundamentally healthy. It seeks to find what is working and uses a magnifying glass to increase awareness of it, so that it can be used more consciously in dealing with present and future difficulties.

Professor Anthony Grant has written 'Successful coaching works on finding solutions. It looks forward not backwards. It asks, "How can we change this?", and "How can we do this better?", not "Why did it happen and who's to blame?"'.[4]

A psychologically healthy person will be effective in many areas of their life most of the time, but will have times when their work causes them concern.

Even the most talented and externally successful of people have times in their life when the demands of their work challenge their capabilities and undermine their confidence. By being given the magnifying glass that a coach holds, they are able to identify answers to how they can increase their performance and regain satisfaction in their work. Many of those answers will be in skills to which they already have access.

It is not appropriate for a manager to involve themselves in therapy, and therefore a key skill is in recognizing when the issue goes beyond their competence or comfort, and other sources of help need to be called on. One gift of a solutions approach is that, because it minimizes problem talk, the risk of a manager being drawn into a 'quasi-therapist' role is reduced.

A solutions approach is not about avoiding problems, but about redirecting energy. Anyone who has been worrying about a performance issue for some while has given much thought to the problem. Their critical inner voice will have reverberated within their internal system – a system that is closed off from others. The limitations of a closed system are that it only allows one person access, and over time the problem becomes a familiar companion. In shifting attention to solutions the coach is bringing something new into the system, in the process of which the problem changes size and shape.

Is coaching mentoring?

Because as a manager you can be expected to coach and mentor, it is important to be able to separate out the two activities.

There are long debates between coaches as to whether the two terms are interchangeable. However, I believe that the two are distinct, and it is important to know when you are operating as one and when as the other. The origins of the term 'mentor' come from Homer's *Odyssey*, where Odysseus left his son Telemachus in the care of his friend and adviser Mentor. As he left on his journey, Odysseus primed Mentor to tell Telemachus everything he knew, so that the young man would be prepared for life. When Mentor believed that his work was done he turned himself into a bird, so that he could fly up to a rafter and watch as Telemachus faced a trial alone. At the heart of mentoring is the idea of transferring learning from a more experienced individual to a less experienced person, because it will support their understanding, learning and achievement.[5] It is played out in work through a less experienced person seeking out a more experienced one who has knowledge and skills they desire in support of their own ambitions. The mentor provides a role model and, for this reason informal mentoring, where the mentee identifies someone who offers them what they believe they need, is often more successful than formal mentoring schemes. Mentoring is often a long-term relationship, involving intermittent contact at key transition points, e.g. when considering a job move or during a transition into a new role. Accounts of successful careers will usually include acknowledgement of mentors who played a part at key stages in their development, because they encouraged them to believe that they could do more than they believed themselves capable of doing, and offered advice to support their ambitions. Government Minister Margaret Beckett, questioned about her career as one of the few women of her generation to reach a Cabinet position, has spoken about the role that more experienced politicians played throughout her career in saying, 'You can do more'. Without those mentors pushing her, she claims her career would never have reached its trajectory.

In contrast, coaching assumes that the knowledge resides in the person seeking help. A coach serves to facilitate the learning of the other person, and may not have any particular expertise relevant to the coachee's issue.

The idea of coaching without expertise is a difficult one for many managers to accept, particularly if they see the role of manager as being justified by having more knowledge and skill than their direct reports.

A graphic example of the difference between coaching and mentoring is told by Tim Gallwey,[6,7] a former tennis coach and now an acclaimed coach to business leaders. He tells of being asked to speak to an orchestra, where their scepticism at the notion of coaching without expertise was palpable. He offered to demonstrate his coaching approach and a tuba player walked to the front. Gallwey knew nothing about tuba playing. He asked the musician to play a section of music, and then asked him what was wrong with the playing. To Gallwey's ears the music had sounded fine. The tuba player reported that there was a 'dirty sound' in the upper register – a term meaningless to Gallwey. He asked the tuba player to play it again without doing anything differently, but simply to be aware of anything he noticed. After the repeat performance, Gallwey simply asked what he had noticed, and the player reported that he noticed that when the sound was 'dirty' his tongue was dry and felt thick. From that one invitation to 'notice', the solution emerged – keep the tongue moist. The musician played the piece again, pronounced that the sound was now 'clean' (although to Gallwey's ears it was no different), and left the stage with the knowledge that he had been coached to enhanced performance.

Because Gallwey knew nothing about tuba playing there was no danger of his offering advice, which he might well have done had he been a musician. As a mentor he would have shared the way in which he had addressed the same difficulty, which may or may not have been valid. Instead, Gallwey helped that musician solve his problem rapidly, through holding up the magnifying glass that was inherent in the question, 'what did you notice?'.

There lies the difference between coaching and mentoring.

Is coaching separate from training?

A third potential confusion is in the relative merits of training and coaching. In organizations there is an on-going act of faith called training. It is the out-come of many personal development plan discussions, and the more costly and prestigious the training programme the greater its value as a reflection of the organizational valuing of the individual. It is also true that most training fails to deliver the expected outcome because, while cost-effective, it cannot focus at the individual level of need. Even the best of training experiences dims from memory, as the return to the workplace too often quickly demotes the action plan into a forgotten folder. Supporting the transfer requires the opportunity to relate the input to real issues that the individual is facing, and having the opportunity to test out practice as distinct from theory. It is here that coaching comes in as a lever to maximize the value of training. One study has shown that the productivity gains from offering coaching in support of training are four times those of training alone.[8]

A manager who builds into their direct reports' personal development plan not just the training, but a commitment to coaching them to put into action the outcomes of the training, has substantively increased the likelihood of learning being transferred into sustainable action.

Solution focused as distinct from problem obsessed

The most often asked question in organizations is 'why?'

- Why are sales not increasing despite a fortune spent on marketing?
- Why are our customers less loyal than they used to be?
- Why does the IT solution never deliver what it promised?

- Why are my people resisting change when I have told them time and time again why it's necessary?
- Why can't they manage poor performance when they have been on numerous courses on giving feedback?

Behind this approach is an implicit belief that if we understand the cause we will have the solution. Asking 'why?' seems both reasonable and a signal of intelligence. It links with the culture of many organizations that values only what can be explained through data and reason. It allows people to challenge thought without having to create anything. It is only when we hold the assumption up to the light that its limitations become clear:

- If I understand why I eat too much will it lead to my eating less? Perhaps, or it may provide an excuse for why I eat too much.
- If I understand why I have a poor relationship with my boss, will it improve? Perhaps, or I may absolve myself from trying to improve it.
- If I understand why the CEO terrifies me – will that lead to my being able to speak out and challenge her in meetings? Possibly, or it may leave me with understanding but without the skills to know how to challenge her.

There is a seductive logic in trying to understand the problem, but it does not necessarily lead to a useful outcome.

In the aftermath of a General Election, every party devotes energy to a post-election analysis of 'why?'. Why they did worse than they had hoped, why their message did not get through, why their traditional voters abandoned them? There is detailed analysis by clever people to explain what has passed. To trust that explanation as the basis for ensuring victory next time is risky. Their analysis may be faulty, and by the next election the problems will be different. More value could lie in looking at what worked well. What differentiated those seats that were unexpectedly won from those that were unexpectedly lost? Which candidates connected with their constituents? Which values connected with the public? What worked? Identifying the resources that are there to be used again is a more fruitful exercise than picking over the bones of what was not there. Interestingly, this thinking lay behind the post-election analysis of Lord Saatchi, the Conservative Party Chairman. Rather than commission more research, he issued a pamphlet that identified those things which historically have been found to underpin successful political campaigns, and which he argued had been overlooked in the last campaign.[9]

The attention paid to the pamphlet was scant. Analysing a problem relentlessly is of more media interest than looking at what has been learnt from history.

The principles of a solution focused approach

Solution-led thinking, in contrast, is less interested in unpicking the problem than in identifying what consistently works and to then developing principles drawn from that evidence; principles drawn from observing what helps people bring about change in their behaviour. It is not theoretical, it is completely pragmatic in its focus on capturing what works, rather than understanding what does not work. The principles are simple, and therefore do not look smart. However, the smartness lies in their skilful application.

They can be summarized as:

■ You don't have to understand the cause of a problem in order to help another person find a solution to it. Just as Gallwey never understood why the tuba player's tongue went dry at certain times in his playing, once he brought it to the player's attention the solution appeared.

■ Focusing on the future creates more useful energy than focusing on the past. We create a story from the past in order to explain. When we look to the future we create possibilities.

■ There is no such thing as 'never' or 'always'. Every problem that a person brings does not happen all the time.

■ If something works, do more of it – there is no simpler message.

■ Equally obviously, but less often recognized, if something isn't working stop doing it.

■ Change comes from small steps, rather than giant goals.

■ People are amazingly resourceful, when you allow them to be.

■ Giving praise for what has been achieved (rather than pointing out what hasn't) reinforces the desired behaviour.

Putting the principles into practice

You don't have to understand the cause of a problem to solve it

A member of staff reports that they find a particular customer difficult. They know it is illogical, because they are older and more experienced than the customer, but when they think of meeting with them they feel nervous and, predictably, meetings do not go well. A problem focused approach would be to probe 'why?'. The conversation could then move into a fascinating exploration of the customer's similarities with a key person in the staff member's past. The staff member could leave the meeting feeling happier for having recognized the similarity, but no more equipped to handle the next meeting any differently. The discussion may simply have magnified the issue by reinforcing the links in their mind between two problematic people.

A solution focused approach would help them find ways of incorporating different behaviours into their encounters with the customer. It could do this by getting them to think of other difficult customers where they have managed to improve the relationship, and identifying what they did to bring about the change. Or, the staff member would be encouraged to think of the best encounter they ever had with the customer and what they did that made that encounter less painful, so that they can replicate the conditions.

The success of the next meeting will then be based on having drawn their attention to resources they can readily access, without them ever needing to understand why the relationship is problematic. In making the meeting more successful than previous meetings, the dynamics of the relationship will have begun to change.

There is no such thing as never and always

When things are not going well we generalize from the specific and, in doing so, create an impaired vision that prevents us seeing the detail of the picture. When a colleague claims they 'never get credit for their work' or they 'always make a mess of giving tough messages', they honestly believe it to be true. Left alone with that self-created reality, they then look to reinforce it through looking for more examples of when their efforts have been overlooked or they have failed to deliver a difficult message clearly.

A solution focused approach looks to challenge thinking so as to ground the reality and widen the vision. It is challenging to ask someone who is focused on the 'never' to think of a time when they did get credit for their efforts (even if it was in another time and place) and how they did that. It is challenging to be asked to find a tough message they have given (no matter how small) that wasn't messed up. It is challenging because it forces the other person to confront the partiality of their unforgiving inner voice; to admit that there is another self who deserves a place in their tool bag, because that self has answers, while the unforgiving voice only sees the difficulties.

If something works do more of it

Self-deprecation is a mainstay of British culture. To claim to have no idea why success has happened is an endearing quality in interviews with the rich and famous. It is used to reduce the distance between them and us, and so increase their attractiveness. In reality, anyone who is successful has developed an effective model of things that they have used time and time again. As a tool for enhancing performance, disingenuousness is severely limited. If we don't know how we do something well then how can we do more of it?

CASE STUDY

George is the CEO of a retail chain. When I met him he described his own childhood as the youngest child in a large family living in poor circumstances, where there was never enough money to live on or space to live in. As a young child observing his older siblings working in low-pay jobs he decided that his life was going to be different, and he observed that success in education was key. At the age of 11 years he saw that being Head Boy at a comprehensive school seemed to offer some advantages, so he looked to see what was needed to become Head Boy. He observed a formula: good academic performance, ability in sports, ability to get on with a wide range of people and to build a relationship with the most senior staff. He consciously addressed each competence and, in due course, became Head Boy. When he left university he applied the same approach to his graduate traineeship in a retail chain. He looked to discover which graduate trainees made the most rapid promotion and modelled their behaviours. He saw that they worked in stores close to the homes of Board members, so he asked for a placement near the home of the Company chairman – knowing he would come into the store on a Saturday. He saw that, even while at the bottom of the chain, they would look to do more than learning the 'rules'. They would do something that left a mark on the store. He saw that they did not separate themselves out from non-graduates and would have a go at anything. He emulated their behaviours and once again recognition came.

George consciously modelled success, and having learnt the approach in his teens he used it over and over again in every new environment he went into.

A solution focused approach has a keen interest in how people have managed to be effective, so that the model can be accessed and used consciously. In asking the questions to understand how success has occurred, a person's own individual model emerges. It will probably not be the model of the person trying to help them but, if the coach has helped them to articulate something that hitherto they have used unconsciously and randomly, the coach has provided a great service.

If something does not work, stop it

This statement seems so obvious that it does not need saying, but Bill O'Hanlon,[10] a solution focused therapist, has observed that the difference between humans and rats is that rats learn from experience. Put a piece of cheese in a maze at the end of tunnel 4 and the first time the rat will go down tunnels 1, 2 and 3 before reaching the cheese. The second time he may repeat this process. Very rapidly he will go directly to tunnel 4, and if the cheese is subsequently moved he will rapidly change his behaviour to locate the correct tunnel.

Contrast this with humans, who do the same thing over and over again whilst expecting different results. Even more bizarrely, when something doesn't work they put even more effort into repeating the same thing.

CASE STUDY
Charlotte, a Sales Director, reported that she worked harder than any of her colleagues, to the point of physical collapse. She did this because she believed that showing she could set herself tougher sales targets than anyone else, and deliver on them through exceptional effort, was the key to her becoming the next MD. The fact that she had already been overlooked for the job three times did not stint her belief in this strategy. Only when it was pointed out to her that more masochism would only bring the same result, did she start to look at alternative strategies.

Once she identified what she could do differently, she gained the MD role within nine months.

A solution focused approach challenges people to recognize what is not working and then identify an action that will move them forward. The action does not need to be large, but in the process of doing it and succeeding, their feelings about themselves and their situation will change.

Great changes come from small steps

A goal focused approach to coaching sees the big stretching goal as the starting point for change. As an American friend once said to me 'If you can conceive it, you can achieve it'. The underpinning belief being that in defining a goal beyond one's immediate grasp, the motivation to reach it will generate the energy and commitment to bring about success.

This is the thinking behind the 'where do you see yourself in five year's time?' interview question. Aside from the fact that it leads to answers that the speaker sees as socially desirable (rather than the truth), it is often the case that the speaker has no idea where they see themselves in five year's time. They have an awareness that the step of joining this company will start a different journey, but where it will lead is unknown. Their energy, for the present, is in achieving that first step.

A solution focused approach looks to help people define what progress will look like from where they are currently standing. In the process of making that move, meaningful goals emerge.

CASE STUDY

Shirley, a long-suffering secretary to a University Professor, announced that she found it difficult to manage her boss, and that her goal was to be assertive. Testing the potential benefits and risks of moving from a 'keen to please' to a 'don't mess with me' approach to a colleague, her confidence about clearly and always stating what was acceptable to her started to collapse. Instead, a starting point of defining one thing she could do differently that felt achievable allowed her to experience herself differently while holding the relationship intact. Based on success in defining some principles for how work was to be given to her, she moved on to defining other aspects of her work, and reviewing the outcome. In the process of seeing that she could take control of her workload without harming her relationship with her boss, and that her confidence increased in the process, a goal to become a Faculty Administrator emerged. Assertiveness delivered in manageable steps was the vehicle through which a motivating goal emerged. If she had stated a goal of being Faculty Administrator at the beginning, in line with a theory that says goals should be 'large and audacious', she would have been so aware of the gap between her present self and the self that she believed she needed to be in order to be promoted, she would have had an excuse for doing nothing. By safely experiencing a self that could take control, new possibilities opened up.

Individuals often come stating a goal, because they believe that is what is expected of them. The challenge for the coach is to hold off from grabbing the goal as an anchor, and to allow the presenting goal to be tested for its resilience before committing to action.

People are wonderfully resourceful

Albert Einstein said, 'Most teachers waste their time by asking questions which are intended to discover what a pupil does not know, whereas the true art of questioning has for its purpose to discover what the pupil knows or is capable of knowing'.

The problem focused approach is interested in identifying where deficiency lies in order that it can be fixed. It is why development plans and development centres focus on filling competence gaps, and rarely look at identifying what the person is already good at and how they could become even better.

A solution focused approach starts from the belief that individuals have their lifetimes' wealth of learning available to them, they just need to be helped to find it through giving them space and support.

Benjamin Zander is the conductor of the Boston Philharmonic Orchestra and teaches annually at the New England Conservatory, a school for talented young musicians who have competed to get one of a small number of places. He has reported[11] how, each week, he would ask the musicians to write a journal in which they recorded the capability they had shown that week – as distinct from their usual focus on what they had failed to do and their technical shortcomings. At first the process was self-conscious, but after a few weeks he noticed that the journals changed and they started writing differently. They acknowledged capability and then identified how it could be used to help them deal with the challenges of the following week.

It was when he provided a means for them to identify their resources that they were able to make the connection to how they could use those resources to enhance their performance.

Give praise and acknowledge success

As a child my mother believed that performance was best encouraged by pointing out what was missing. With the best of loving intents, she would point out that 18 out of 20 meant that there were two things I had not addressed properly, or that coming second in an exam meant if only I had tried harder I could have been first. The intent was to motivate, the outcome was an internal collapse as the inner voice shouted, 'I will never be good enough'.

In contrast, solution focused thinking gives praise and acknowledgement for what the other person has achieved. It is praise beyond the automatic 'well done', but rather acknowledgement that tries to help the other person understand 'how they did it'.

CASE STUDY

Sophie came to coaching with her own 'never and always' story, which said 'I am hopeless at interviews'. She also had plenty of evidence to back up her assessment. Through coaching she was helped to understand what of herself she could take to interviews that would help her, so that she did not feel out of control whenever she sat in front of an interview panel. Her success at her next interview was not in getting the job – which she did not – but in experiencing herself differently in a situation where hitherto she had programmed how she would be. The praise I gave Sophie was for having taken the risk of being different, and the acknowledgement I gave her was for the specific things she had done to prepare herself, so that those behaviours were magnified for her and could be used again.

When reading these principles, they may seem too simple to be effective. Particularly if you value your analytical skills, to accept that it is not necessary to understand the cause of a difficulty in order to bring about change seems counter-intuitive. This has been a regular challenge made to the pioneers of this approach. However, they can point to their own experience based on 30 years work that by using these principles, individuals need only a small number of sessions to make desired changes to major difficulties, and that the learning sticks.[12]

Principles are good as a compass guide to your behaviour when coaching, but knowing when and how to apply them within a conversation requires a structure.

The remaining chapters provide that structure. It is a structure that you can use whether the conversation lasts for five minutes or ninety. At the beginning it will feel like a strait-jacket, because it will make you conscious of what you are doing. Moving from step to step will feel clumsy, in much the same way as changing gears is a self-conscious process when learning to drive. Each impending gear change brings a tug of anxiety. With practice, when to change gear seeps into your unconscious, so that you access it without thinking and apply it with skill. Similarly in coaching, with practice you will move seamlessly around the framework, using whichever part is helpful to reaching an outcome.

The structure that will support you in having successful coaching conversations with your staff is STARTED.

STARTED

S   *Set up*
T   *Tangibles*
A   *Assumptions*
R   *Reality bites*
T   *Targeting*
E   *Emergent solutions*
D   *Delivery*

Each letter will form the basis of a chapter, where you will be offered tools to help in the management of that stage, and examples of how the tools can be applied.

Each letter has a strong link with the principles we have established for solution focused coaching and with the skills that effective coaches use.

Structural Stage	Coaching Skill
Set Up Establishing the purpose of the conversation and creating the conditions in the coach and the coachee for a helpful conversation	*Support for Thought*
Tangibles Allowing the person to define the situation as they see it, and expanding the perspectives from which they see it	*Support for Thought* *Challenge for Thought*
Assumptions Testing out the assumptions that they bring to the situation, and the limitations these are placing on them	*Challenge for Thought*
Reality Bites Grounding their thinking through clarifying when the problem does and does not happen. Helping them to see the situation from other perspectives than their own	*Challenge for Thought*
Targeting Identifying the goal that is appropriate for them. Enabling them to revisit their original purpose and reconsider its value in the light of the coaching conversation	*Support for Thought*
Emergent Solutions The identification by the coachee of the 'right' solution for them at this time. Helping them to highlight the skills, knowledge and experience they have within them that they can bring to the situation	*Support for Thought*
Delivery Scoping the size of the solution to be delivered. Learning from failure and supporting success	*Challenge for Action* *Support for Action*

Figure 4.1   The STARTED structure

As the conversation progresses, as a Manager Coach you will be moving through the STARTED structure, but you will also be moving within yourself as you shift from each of the four skill areas in response to the other's need. A coach who easily offers support for thought could miss out on the possibilities that emerge when challenge is brought into the picture. A coach who rushes to challenge thought without addressing the need to support thought at the beginning may quickly identify a target for coaching, but in the process miss the point. A coach who encourages the emergence of solutions but does not address the challenge of delivery will have wasted their time. Coaching is a dance, and developing your core skills within a structure will enable you to deliver those skills whether you are operating at the pace of a waltz or a salsa.

Summary

This chapter has differentiated coaching from other forms of helping and performance development. It has argued for a solution focused approach as the basis for effective and time-efficient coaching within organizations. In doing so it has:

- introduced the principles of solution focused thinking
- laid out the STARTED framework for structuring conversations
- linked that framework to the coach's application of both support and challenge.

References

1. de Shazer, S. (1988) *Clues Investigating Solutions in Brief Therapy.* Norton.
2. de Shazer, S. (1994) *Words Were Originally Magic.* Norton.
3. de Jong, P. and Berg, I.K. (2002) *Interviewing for Solutions.* Thomson Learning.
4. Greene, J. and Grant, A.B. (2003) *Solution-Focused Coaching.* Pearson Education.
5. Megginson, D. and Garvey, B. (2004) Odysseus, Telemachus and Mentor: stumbling into, searching for and signposting the road to desire. *The International Journal of Mentoring and Coaching*, II, 1, July. Available on line at http://www.emccouncil.org
6. Gallwey, T.W. (2005) *Keynote Address: The Inner Game of Work.* International Coach Federation European Annual Conference.
7. Gallwey, T.W. (2000) *The Inner Game of Work.* Orion Business.
8. Olivero, G., Bane, K.D. and Kopelman, R.E. (1997) Executive Coaching as a transfer of learning tool: effects on productivity in a public agency. *Personnel Management*, 26 (4), 461–69.
9. Saatchi, M. (2005) *If This is Conservatism, I am a Conservative.* Centre for Policy Studies.
10. O'Hanlon, W.H. (2000) *Do One Thing Differently.* Perennial.
11. Stone Zander, R. and Zander, B. (2000) *The Art of Possibility.* Harvard Business Press.
12. Gingerich, W.J. and Eisengart, S. (2000) Solution focused brief therapy: a review of the outcome research. *Family Process*, 39 (4), 477–98.

5

Set Up

The beginning is the most important part of the work.
Plato

Without looking, describe what is on the back of a £10 note. Logical thinkers will start with the number 10; the watermark; the signature of the head cashier – but is that on the back or front? The visual thinkers will see a head of a famous man – but is it Shakespeare, Darwin or Robert Stephenson? You may remember a bird – but which bird? You will remember the colour brown but what other colours are used? Find a £10 note and see just how much you have missed. There is a wealth of information conveyed on that piece of paper: the hummingbird sniffing at a flower; the magnifying glass showing up the stamens of flowers; a galleon sailing towards the viewer; a compass; the head of Charles Darwin and colours from across the spectrum. The reason it is unlikely you have recalled all this detail is that you don't need to. From the time you started to manage your own money, you learnt to scan notes for the minimum amount of information that you needed to ensure you handed over, and were handed back, the correct note.

The ability to scan is a useful one, it minimizes effort. In our daily lives, we scan to quickly read situations. We scan people in order to assess their age, approachability, socio-economic group, lifestyle and likeness to ourselves. Our accuracy rate will depend on our level of observational and intuitive skill. The same approach transfers into our working lives. Someone new comes into our work team, we pay close interest in the first few weeks and months as we try and assess their strengths and weaknesses, their ambitions and motivations. When we think we have enough information we switch from observing to scanning. We develop a general view that we access when we are judging whether to give a piece of work to A or B, or whether to ask C or D to stand in for us at a meeting. It allows us to make decisions quickly. However, if we are to position ourselves as offering coaching to our staff, it is important to switch off our scanner and become an active observer.

To observe is to invite

Scanning allows us to take in enough information to serve our own purposes. Observation asks that you look at the other person and use the information you receive to help them.

Paul notices that while Richard is happy to air his views on a one to one basis, he rarely speaks out in meetings, even when the issue is one that Paul knows he has a view on.

In his scanning mode, Paul uses that data to raise issues with Richard informally, and to minimize the number of meetings he invites him to.

In his observational mode he feeds back to Richard, immediately after a particularly difficult meeting, that he has noticed that Richard said very little today, and wonders if he feels uncomfortable airing his views to large groups. Richard admits that he feels that by the time he has the confidence to speak out the agenda had moved on, so there is no point in speaking.

Paul is able to use that feedback as an opening to coach, through asking 'would you like some help in how to get your message across?'.

Similarly, Rosemary has a very self-confident graduate trainee who is always pushing to get profile through taking on work that brings visibility. With her scanner, Rosemary gives him opportunities that she holds back from the less confident graduates in her group. When she sees him coming back from a visit to an external client looking downhearted, rather than ignoring the data, she decides to test out her observation. 'You don't seem your usual self, has something happened at the meeting?'. When he reveals that he felt he had made a fool of himself in front of a Senior Executive by talking too much, she could simply bat it away with a, 'Well, we all make mistakes' or 'Don't worry, he won't remember'. Instead, she says, 'I would be willing to help you think through how you could have handled the meeting differently, if that would be helpful'.

In both cases, the individual has the choice as to whether they respond. Similarly, the manager has the choice as to whether they ignore the issue, observe and direct, or observe and offer to coach. Paul could have observed and directed, saying 'You don't contribute enough in meetings, you need to speak out more'. Rosemary could have said 'You need to curb your own enthusiasms and recognize when you are the most junior person in a meeting'. Such advice would have signalled their own positions, but would not necessarily have been received as well-intentioned. Instead, both offered an invitation, based on using their observations, and both couched the invitation in a way that made it clear that control over what happened next lay with the employee, not their manager.

The starting point of Set Up is to shift from scanner to observer, and to use those observations to test out if the other person is ready to be coached. Readiness and timeliness are key. If Rosemary makes the offer the following week or even the following day, the graduate may well have restored their sense of equilibrium, discounted the Executive as an 'old fart' and continue to behave in the same way in a similar meeting. If Paul made the offer just before a meeting, Richard would probably have dismissed it, or spent the whole meeting feeling even more self-conscious. Instead, by using their observational skills both managers are able to work with the gift that timeliness gives, i.e. it provides an immediacy that means that the thoughts and the emotions surrounding it are both more raw and more accurate.

Talk to the graduate weeks after the event, and he will have constructed an alternate version of the experience. A version that protects his self-image as the confident fast-tracker. Talk to Richard about the meeting some time after, and he will have constructed a version that ignores any contribution he made at the time, because of his focus on seeing his own inadequacies when speaking in a group. With distance, we rewrite our stories to fit with the character we have created for ourselves. When we hear the story soon after it occurs, it has not had time to be reworked, so it is less neat in the telling. In that messiness, a more valuable picture emerges.

The payoff that comes with using observation to make a timely coaching offer is that it provides a tight focus for the discussion. Paul is not offering to help Richard become an extrovert. He is not offering to help with a whole range of other situations in which Richard may paralyse himself because of his need to have the argument perfected in his head before he speaks. He is offering to help him find a way in which he can contribute more readily in a specific situation, so that his views are taken account of and his abilities are recognized. The potential benefit is that once Richard finds he can be different in one context, he can find ways of extending that approach to others. Rosemary is not offering to help her graduate to understand why he has the need to assert himself when speaking with authority figures. She is offering to help him recognize what he was wanting to achieve in that situation, so that he can identify more appropriate behaviours for achieving that purpose. The learning from that conversation may help him in other situations where he is dealing with a more senior person, without Rosemary ever being involved.

Coaching that is offered at the right time in a way that focuses attention on developing specific solutions that are right for that person allows for the creation of ripples, of which the manager may never be aware. Without that observation, the possibility of those ripples would not have been realized. A timely observation is a pebble that is offered to the other person. If they pick it up and use it to break the surface, its impact can spread far wider than they ever anticipated.

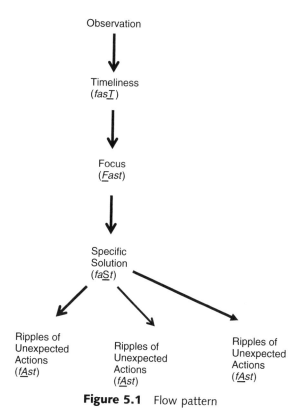

Figure 5.1 Flow pattern

Figure 5.1 looks at this as a flow pattern.

CASE STUDY

Jan had been promoted from being a part-time receptionist to being the full-time supervisor of the reception team. She was now responsible for women who previously she had seen as friends, and she was struggling with how to bring some discipline to their working arrangements. They dismissed any attempt to focus their performance, with excuses about the failings of everyone around them or the demands of their domestic life. It was a formula that hooked Jan every time. The pebble came when Jan's manager saw Jan sitting on reception when she knew that Jan had deadlines to meet on other pieces of work. She also noticed that Jan looked less than happy. The comment, 'I would not have expected to see you on reception today, and you look as though you don't want to be there either', allowed Jan to explode with rage. She felt she had been forced to act as the receptionist because her colleague had phoned in saying she had forgotten it was her son's sports day. Jan, knowing the colleague was a single parent, had found it impossible to make more than the mildest of protests before she found herself being thanked profusely for her understanding. Her manager then made the offer, 'would you like some help in finding a way of dealing with this when she comes in tomorrow?'. Jan accepted the offer while explaining the impossibility of ever getting anything to change because they knew she was 'a soft touch'. Her manager ignored the wider issue of being a soft touch, and focused Jan on thinking about her situation from a wider perspective than friendship. From this Jan was able to develop what she felt she was able to say that would prevent a similar situation arising. The experience of hearing herself say things to her direct report that she would not have thought it possible to say was powerful. Finding that the other person accepted them was revelatory and started the creation of a ripple effect. Rather than absorbing their moans, she found herself challenging them to state what they wanted, rather than what they did not want. When she heard them speaking about personal issues in reception she suggested they agree a code of behaviour that would fit with being a professional reception service. From that one conversation with her manager she started to build an identity of herself as a professional supervisor, rather than the receptionist that got lucky.

OBSERVATIONAL EXERCISE

To test out the power of observation as the starting point of coaching, set yourself the following exercise.

Week one

Commit to observing a member of staff when you are together. As a detached viewer, look at what information you pick up from them: their mood, their energy, their commitment, their confidence. What do you notice that is not expressed? You need do nothing other than observe, and notice whether it gives you information that is useful or that normally you would discount.

Caution: this is not an exercise in stalking or professional detective work, just be your normal self but with the mindfulness of paying more attention than you normally do to the information you are receiving.

Week two

Continue to observe, and look for an opening where your observation could be a useful link with their performance, e.g. notice their reaction to a setback; to feedback; to other people. Throw out a pebble through testing whether your observation is correct, e.g. 'You seemed disappointed by . . .', 'I sensed you were feeling left out of . . .', 'I noticed that you . . .'. Don't worry if your observation is not totally accurate. If you are accurate they will feel validated, if you are inaccurate they will correct you, and you will learn something.

You don't have to make an offer to coach at this point – simply gain practice in taking the risk of stating your observations, and seeing what follows.

Creating the space

A well-timed and accurate observation resulting in an offer of coaching that is accepted, leads to the question of when and where the conversation is going to occur, and are you ready for it?

The principle of FAST coaching is that it works best when it is timely. This could mean that the invitation is offered whilst standing in a corridor, at the photocopier or in an airport lounge. Conventional coaching would suggest that coaching takes place in a quiet space without interruptions; that it mirrors the conditions found in a therapist's office, where an allocated amount of time is given to the discussion; that there are no distractions and the commitment is to meet regularly. Does this mean that coaching can only take place behind closed doors and has to be a regular commitment?

From the perspective of a manager who is trying to build coaching skills into their daily lives, the answer is 'No'. It is possible to 'coach on the hoof', but the conditions have to be present that allow for attention to be given.

Training in interview skills includes advice on ensuring that the space where the interview is conducted is free of clutter, phone calls and other interruptions. Creating a space away from the demands of work is a signal of giving full attention to the interviewee. It is a means of enabling the interviewer to empty their minds of the competing activities that await them on their desks, in their email and at the end of the phone.

The same is true of the manager who makes an offer of coaching attention. They need to be sure that the conditions are present for both the coach and the coachee to set up well together. From the perspective of the coachee, they need to feel comfortable in the place where the conversation is taking place. For the coach they need to know that they have emptied their minds of everything except the need to focus on that other person.

Creating the space is both a literal and a metaphorical exercise. The right space can be in the corridor. The right space can be in the formal meeting room. It needs, however, to work for both people. One person may be comfortable in the corridor because it allows them to talk about the issue immediately and it is that immediacy they value. That may not work for their manager, who is aware of all the other people passing by as they speak. Booking a formal meeting room a week ahead for an hour may work for the manager, because they know that that time will be devoted to nothing else, whereas the staff member may find that their anxiety increases with a time lapse.

There are no right and wrong answers about creating the space to talk, except that both parties have to feel comfortable with it. The employee and manager who felt happy talking about a problem in store layout in front of the chill display area (see Chapter 1), would not have achieved a better result if they had removed themselves to the manager's office. Had one or other of them felt unhappy having the conversation in a public place the outcome would not have been reached so quickly.

Formality can be a barrier to coaching or it can signal that the person is being taken seriously. Informality can be liberating or an excuse for a lack of focus. The coach has to establish with the other person what will work best in that moment.

CASE STUDY

Ryan works as a lawyer. He had been receiving coaching because he had taken on a managerial role within the practice and was finding it hard to let go of ways of working that were helpful as a professional specialist but got in the way of motivating and managing others. He had had a number of coaching sessions in the meeting room of the practice – the only dedicated private space available. The next time he entered the room his coach noticed that he seemed agitated. She fed back this observation, and he began a tirade about how he was feeling about the place and the thoughts he was having about wanting to escape from it all. Picking up the phrase 'escape', she made the invitation 'would you like to escape from this building for our session today?'. He leapt at the idea with such rapidity that she knew she was right. She allowed him to decide where they should go, and he chose a local park. She was unsure whether it would work, but decided to go along with it. Once sitting down in open space, he started to open up in a way he had never done within the formal environment. Seeing the difference it was making, she decided to ignore her own concerns about the level of noise and visual distraction around and simply focus on him. The outcome was a session of such a different quality to previous sessions, made visible in the actions he took subsequently, that she knew she had made the right decision.

Clearing the internal space

For managers, clearing the internal space is as important as clearing the diary. It is important because, if it is not cleared, the other person knows. Anyone who has a child will have experienced those times where, while physically present, the parental mind is roving elsewhere: running through the things they have to do, the things they would be doing if they were not pushing the swing, playing football or role-playing a fantasy game. They will also know that the child reads very quickly when they are not totally present and either increases the level of demand they place on them in order to crowd out competing thoughts, or moves off to find someone whom they read as being more available.

Adults are no different, though they may lack the truthfulness of the child in how they deal with it. They are unlikely to challenge you about your lack of attention, but they will recognize that you are not fully engaged and will hold back from fully engaging with you in return. Since you are their boss they are likely to read it as a signal to quickly bring the conversation to an end, so that you are free to focus back on your competing interests. As an investment of your time, it has a low return. Better to give ten minutes total space and help something change for the other person, than to give five minutes insufficient attention with no outcome. If you make the offer to coach and it is accepted, you have the responsibility of clearing your internal space if it is going to be an effective use of your time. If you cannot clear that space then it is not the right time to coach.

Strangely, one of the side effects of a FAST coaching approach can be that when the conversation happens in the moment, it is easier to give full attention because you are both committed to the issue. The manager notices that the staff member is struggling with something, they feed in their observation and it is received as accurate. The manager makes an offer to coach and it is accepted. Suddenly they are both partners in the same dance and the other demands of the day fall away. Contrast this with an identification of a coaching need that comes from a formal appraisal discussion. Time is set aside and, as the allocated time comes, the manager is thinking of all the other things that they could easily do with that hour: the report that if it isn't written today will have to be done over the weekend; the phone calls they should return by the end of the day; the 200 unanswered emails.

Establishing purpose

Having made the offer to coach and it being accepted, there is a powerful instinct to jump straight in and ask the coachee to identify their goal.

Goal setting is the assumed starting point of most coaching. You go to a gym and the personal trainer asks you what your goals are, in order to put together a schedule. You attend a course and you are expected to define your learning goals at the outset. You spend annual appraisal discussions setting goals based around the SMART mantra of specificity, measurability, achievability, relevance and time boundaries.

Goals are good. Goals are motivating. 'If you can dream it, you can achieve it', is the language of self-help manuals. The most commonly applied coaching model in UK organizations starts from goals.[1] Goals are important. The limitations of goals are that often they are premature. There is a pressure to be able to state the goal before both parties are clear on what the correct goal is.

When asked to state a goal early in a conversation, most people will state a goal that they think the other person will view as socially acceptable.

On day one of a course to develop skills in a particular coaching approach, I was paired with a young attractive man in his early 20s. When asked to state his goals he expressed ones linked to applying the learning to his work. Later in the week I coached him, and we returned to the issue of his goals. This time he was far more hesitant, before eventually saying, 'I don't know if I can say this to you'. 'Try me', I offered. Embarrassed, he said, 'The real reason I want to learn this stuff is so that I can be irresistible to women'. Could he have admitted that on day one? – unlikely. He had to establish that I was a safe person to disclose to before he could name his strongest motivator to learning.

Because goals are the motivational currency of organizational performance, people feel that they have to be able to state a goal as the starting point for change. The logic states, identify the goal, identify the gap between current reality and the goal, identify the means to reduce the barriers to achieving the goal and take action.

EXAMPLE

Christine knows that she finds it difficult to say 'No' to requests for her help when they come from someone that she likes. She sets a goal of being assertive with her colleagues. She identifies that, at present, she rarely if ever shows any signs of dissent to any request, no matter how unreasonable she feels it is. She recognizes that the barrier is a fear of being disliked, so tries to convince herself that if being assertive means risking losing your friends that is what she must do. She starts saying 'No' loudly and frequently, and pretty soon she finds she has few requests made of her. She has achieved her goal. However, somewhere in the process of achieving the goal she has missed the point, because she never established what her purpose was. Now that her days are spent on her own work with no expectation from her colleagues that she should help them out, she strangely feels no better about herself, although she has learnt assertiveness skills.

A more useful starting point for Christine would have been to establish her purpose in wanting to be more assertive. Is it to reduce the number of social interactions she has? Is it to have more time to focus on key areas of her role? Is it to signal that she is not a push-over? Is it to develop skills that will help her get wider recognition for her work? Until Christine is clear on the purpose of changing her behaviour, the application of the skill of assertion will risk being misplaced. When we start from a goal, it helps provide us with a structure of certainty, but often we do not understand the implications of the goal we have set.

Rather than focusing on goals, individuals in the Set Up stage are helped by being allowed 'fuzzy vision'.[2] Fuzzy vision validates people for not knowing precisely what they want, by encouraging them to talk about how they would like things to be different rather than setting a precise outcome.

Consider the difference between goal setting and allowing for 'fuzzy vision' in the case of Richard, the reluctant meetings attendee.

The manager observes that Richard is reluctant to speak out in meetings and offers to help. They start from the question 'What is your goal for yourself in meetings?'

Richard, recognizing a SMART approach when he sees it and not wanting to let his manager down, replies, 'I would like to be able to contribute to all meetings that I attend within three months'.

The manager now guides Richard into setting subgoals for his contribution to forthcoming meetings so that, at the end of 3 months, they can judge progress.

Both understand the logic of this process, and Richard may even hit this performance measure, but has he achieved his real target?

It is possible that Richard is unclear at the beginning what his goal is. He knows there is something about him and meetings that does not work well, but he does not know how to change it. Being asked a 'fuzzy' question, 'What would be a good way of spending our time in looking at you and meetings?', allows for the conversation to take any number of directions. Richard may:

- want to think through what he does in meetings that makes him feel more and more marginal
- want to get feedback on how he comes across in meetings
- want to think through how he could go to meetings with a more positive mindset
- want to find ways of interrupting the flow of conversation so that he is heard at the right time.

He may be at an even 'fuzzier' stage if he has not, until that moment, considered that he could be any different in his behaviours. His vision could be as blurred as, 'I would just like to talk through with someone how I behave when I am in large groups, to help me get some perspective on it'.

Allowing for 'fuzzy vision' is about allowing the individual to define the purpose of the conversation, without forcing their attention on goals.

'Fuzzy vision' is something that people in organizations believe is unallowable, since displaying less than 20/20 certainty risks being read as inadequacy. The value of 'fuzzy vision' is that it allows for looking at things without focusing on one outcome. A coach who can allow for 'fuzziness' is not wasting time, they are encouraging the individual to explore until they find the right goal.

Herminia Ibarra, writing on the process of career change,[3] has argued strongly that career planning that follows the process of identifying abilities, strengths and values, and matching them with opportunities, has unarguable logic but often leads people to unsatisfactory outcomes. This approach assumes that humans are creatures of pure reason and will therefore want change to be an extension of what they already know. In reality people often don't know what they want, but they do know what they no longer want. It is only through the process of being allowed 'fuzzy vision' that they can think about themselves more openly and honestly, and in doing so find an outcome that is right for them.

At some point, goals do become important (see Chapter 9), and research on the value of goals conducted over 30 years[4] has shown that:

- goals that are specific and difficult lead to the highest performance
- commitment to goals is most critical when the goal is difficult and specific
- high commitment is attained when the goal is important to you.

However, getting to meaningful specificity, gaining real commitment and wanting to set oneself difficult goals comes from being allowed to define real purpose through a tolerance of 'fuzziness'.

Agreeing purpose: not setting goals

At the Set Up stage of the coaching process, the establishment of the purpose of the conversation is the responsibility of the coach. They do this through asking questions such as:

- How would you like to spend this time?
- What would be a good use of the next 20 minutes?
- What would make this conversation worthwhile for you?
- What would you like to be different after talking this through together?

These are questions that allow for goal setting but they are equally accepting of 'fuzzy' responses. They are questions that place the agenda in the hands of the other person. They are also asked in order to enable the Manager Coach to assess if they can buy into that purpose.

The question 'how would you like to spend this time?' leading to a response such as, 'I would like to talk about how my personal life is affecting my ability to do what you are expecting of me', allows the Manager Coach to consider whether they can buy into that purpose.

- They may be comfortable with the disclosure, but want to put boundaries around the conversation.

    I know your personal life is impacting on work, so I am happy to hear more, provided that we also use the time to find ways of keeping your work on track.

- They may be very uncomfortable with the bringing together of the two elements and want to separate them out.

    Your personal life is obviously affecting your work, and I am happy to help you find a way of getting support for those issues, but it is not an area I feel confident in handling with you – so what would be a good use of our time together?

- They may be very comfortable with the content, but need to remind themselves of their purpose.

    I appreciate your feeling you can talk with me about things outside of work. I am happy to listen to you, but what you need to know is that I have no skills in helping you resolve those issues. That may help you decide how you want to use this session.

The staff member is allowed 'fuzzy vision', but equally it is important that the Manager Coach has clarity about what their purpose is in the conversation and manages that responsibility.

Getting clarity on what both sides can expect from the conversation is a foundation of the Set Up stage.

PURPOSE EXERCISE

Focus on yourself. Consider a goal you have set yourself either at work or in life generally, e.g. I am going to get a promotion within a year; I am going to learn to play the guitar. Ask yourself the purpose of that goal. What would it mean for you if you achieved it? Could that purpose be achieved in a number of other ways? How important is the specificity of the goal, or is it more useful to recognize the purpose of the goal so that a wider range of options are available?

Listening with intent

In taking the first step of making an observation, you have shown that you are listening to the other person, and your listening has come from multiple senses.

Your observation may have come from visually listening to their body language, their facial expression or their degree of eye contact. Your observation may have been led less by the content of what they said but by listening to their tone of voice and its speed. You may even have listened to your own feelings and taken the risk of expressing them as a way of opening up the observation.

Similarly, in agreeing purpose, you have shown that you are willing to listen through allowing them to create the agenda for the conversation, and that not having a clear outcome is permitted. Before the conversation has even begun, you have shown that you are there to listen, and that you are willing to support their thought processes.

The core of the conversation that follows, wherever it takes place, will succeed or fail to the degree that you as the coach are able to listen with intent. That requires that you apply your listening senses for very different purposes than are required in the daily maelstrom of work. At work we listen to avoid; listen to compete; listen to compute; listen to rescue; listen to solve. Let's look at each of these in turn.

Listen to avoid

We hear what someone is saying or not saying and we choose to pay it no attention. It's what Americans call 'the elephant in the corner', and Canadians label as the 'moose under the table'. At its least important, we hear someone explaining the catastrophes that happened before they got to work that day, and we make no comment, because our focus is on not allowing them to use their bad start to the day as an excuse for how they are going to perform in the presentation that is about to start.

More critically, we listen and recognize what is happening within our team or organization, but it remains un-named and therefore unresolved until it blows up and has to be named. When the Accident Investigation report was written on the 1986 Columbia space shuttle disaster, the immediate cause of the accident was foam on the wing during lift off. The underlying cause was a safety culture within NASA that would only listen to people according to rank. NASA values stated that it was expertise not rank that mattered, but everyone knew the truth that rank won over expertise, and no one had challenged it.[5] Managers often know what the problem is with an individual, but avoid listening to data because to acknowledge it will mean bringing the elephant out of its corner and having to do something, rather than hoping the elephant carries on sleeping.

Listen to compete

We listen to one another to the degree necessary in order to get information from which we can compete. We listen in order to compete in our 'ain't life awful around here' stories, and we listen to get data that allows us to 'top' others' achievements or disasters. It's part of the fabric that forms the underpinning of much social interaction within work. We are not concerned about how awful or great it was for them, we are interested in how their story provides an opening for our story.

Listening to compute

We listen to get enough information that feeds into our agenda. We want to be given the good news but not the bad, because that might derail our attention. We want the facts but not the emotions surrounding them, because dealing with emotions takes time. Those managers with a preference for concrete thinking and 'getting on with the job', are irritated when the other person wants to delay handing over the data by requiring social interaction as a pre-requisite to doing business. One of the skills of successful leaders is that in conversation they are scanning the input of the other speaker to test out what in the content maps onto an issue they are currently concerned with. In any conversation they will engage with only a small part of it, because only a small part will be of use to them. They will quickly show their irritation when they feel that speaker's relevant database is used up, or it is information they have heard before.

Listen to rescue

If we are feeling listeners we listen for the feelings behind the words of the other, and imagine we are that person. From this listening position, we want to make life easier for the other person through rescuing them from the difficulty – just as Jan found it impossible to challenge her errant receptionist when she imagined what it must be like to be unable to attend a child's sports day. The problem with listening to rescue is that it denies the other person the possibility of finding their own solution, and it creates a pattern that will play out again and again.

Listen to solve

Someone brings an issue to us and we hear in their input that they need us to solve the problem for them. Given the attractiveness of being the holder of solutions, we offer them without checking if the other person wanted an answer or simply space to talk. We then feel aggrieved when our solution is not appreciatively applied. Steven Covey has written of the wisdom of seeking 'to understand first then seek to be understood',[6] but the desire to make others understand what they need to do through sharing our wisdom is often irresistible.

When I have asked any group of managers to talk for five minutes about an issue that is important to them, while their partner listens, it is rare for five minutes of listening to occur without any advice being given. Often, the advice will be offered within ninety seconds of them starting to talk. When I then ask how long it was before they were offering advice, participants will apologize if they failed to solve their partner's issue, and simply listened, while those who offered their wisdom will be confident that ninety seconds of listening was all they needed before they knew the other person's situation sufficiently well to offer their insights.

We can listen to solve if the issue is strictly informational – Where do I find out about? Who is responsible for? How much is . . . ? When do I need to . . . ? Informational listening is helpful when the employee is new to their role, but most issues that able individuals bring to their managers do not fall into that category.

Listening with intent means two type listening

The listening that a Manager Coach uses is qualitatively different from the listening habits of daily life. It is listening in order to help the other person achieve a change related to their purpose. This requires:

- listening to understand content
- listening to understand the other person's values and beliefs
- listening to understand the emotion they bring
- listening to understand their personality as it impacts on this issue
- listening to understand the energy they attach to the issue.

Listening with intent is an iceberg activity (Figure 5.2).

Each type of listening is necessary for a coaching conversation, and each needs to be managed by the coach so that the balance between the two is helpful to the other person.

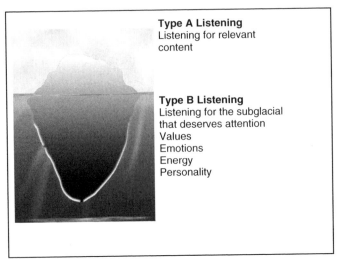

Type A Listening
Listening for relevant
content

Type B Listening
Listening for the subglacial
that deserves attention
Values
Emotions
Energy
Personality

Figure 5.2 The two types of listening

Type A listening

Type A listening is listening above the water line. It encompasses the skills that are typically taught on interpersonal development courses. It is listening where the listener signals that they are giving the other person their full attention. They do this by matching their body language and matching voice tone.

Matching their body language

The listener signals that they are in rapport with the other person through matching their body language. If the speaker shows that they are more comfortable standing up then the listener stands up. If the speaker sits in a relaxed position with their legs crossed, then the listener will do the same. If the speaker is a straight-back, feet-firmly-planted sort of person, then the listener will make sure they match their body accordingly. Although this may seem self-conscious for the coach, the evidence is that, done subtly, it is read as a signal of matching by the coachee, and helps trust and rapport building.[7] The modelling of the other does not have to be exact, but showing similarity in how you position your body will be read positively.

Just as body matching contributes to the sense that the coach is in congruence with them, matching level of eye contact does the same. Giving and avoiding eye contact as a signal of giving or withholding listening is one of the earliest social skills that we learn as children. In listening with intent, the giving of eye contact is crafted to read how much eye contact the other person is comfortable with, and then matching it. Full-on, eyes open attention can be disconcerting rather than encouraging. The person who is uncomfortable with a lot of direct eye contact will read, if subconsciously, that the coach is in rapport with them if they reduce the amount of direct visual attention they give.

MATCHING BODY LANGUAGE EXERCISE

Because body language listening is given far less attention than other aspects of Type A listening, it is likely to be a less-developed aspect of a Manager Coach's tool kit.

Experiment with matching with others' body language. It is a game that can be easily played on public transport. Focus on someone within eye contact and notice their body position. Model it. As they change position, leave a gap of several seconds and then change yours in response. Repeat this a number of times and then change your position and notice if they then follow you. *Caution:* if they clearly have noticed your modelling, then abandon the exercise in case they read your desire to learn as a desire to ridicule.

Once you are comfortable with changing body position subtly, experiment whilst at work and notice whether the conversation is influenced by your matching of the other's body language.

As a final check, once you can see that body matching helps build rapport with another person, deliberately mis-match body language and notice if it impacts on the interaction.

Matching voice tone

The development of informal language by teenagers, known only to them and used to exclude adults, is more than the sharing of a 'patois'. Listen to a group of young males out for the night and, while their words may be incomprehensible, each person will mirror the level and speed at which the words are spoken by the others. In doing so they are signalling to themselves and to those outside their circle that they have a united identity.

The ability to match voice with another person is a valuable aid to building a sense of connection. Within a coaching conversation the listener hears the speed and level of voice and matches with it. If the speaker is a rapid streamer, the listener may need to rev up their natural speed. If the coach is a torrent speaker they will need to slow down to match with someone who flows more slowly. Similarly, if the speaker has a soft voice, the attentive listener will hear that and adjust their levels accordingly. If the speaker is a fog horn, the coach will need to 'amp up' their normal level. The speaker who is hesitant in their speech patterns will respond to a listener who presents their ideas with some hesitancy. The speaker who shows they need silence to help their thinking will feel valued by a listener who allows them that silence. For a Manager Coach, allowing silence can be difficult. It is a rare occurrence in working conversations; yet allowing silence beyond the comfort point of the listener is a powerful means of signalling the rapport from which disclosure comes.

MATCHING VOICE TONE EXERCISE

Talk with someone with whom you have a good relationship, and observe how well you match with each other in how you use the speed and tone of your voices. What is the effect of that matching on how you communicate and your feelings about the conversation? Experiment with allowing silence through counting to ten internally before following up on a point they make, and notice what emerges when you allow that silence.

Identify someone who speaks very differently from you and consciously move your pattern to more closely match theirs. This will need to be done subtly, so it is best to find someone where the gap is not so large that your sudden change of style will be transparent. Notice any changes that you see or feel as a result of the change in how you use your voice with them.

The core skills of Type A listening

The focused Type A listening skills that underpin coaching are the same as those used by people who are described by others as 'good listeners'. Watch what they do and you will see them encouraging; clarifying; summarizing; reflecting; empathizing.

Encouraging

This provides regular signals that the good listener wants the person to continue, because they are engaged in what they are being told. Those signals may be visual – nods of the head, smiling, body matching. They can also be verbal, providing they are intentional. A series of 'Mm's and 'Aha's' can be genuine encouragement or a signal of zoned out listening.

In coaching, encouraging listening is about enabling the other person to tell as much as is helpful to the coaching purpose – but no more. It is not coaching to simply leave space that the other person can fill. Encouraging listening is focused on unearthing what is relevant through such interventions as:

- Tell me more about . . .
- What else?
- What haven't you said so far?
- I value your openness in saying that – is there anything more you want to say about it?

While encouragement is a means by which we signal to the other person that we value and validate them, as a Manager Coach your encouragement is also about helping them to focus on what is important.

Clarifying

Good listeners make sure that they understand what they are being told, rather than assuming it. Being asked to clarify is a means by which a coach signals that they want to be sure that they have got it right. When someone is given the opportunity to talk about themselves they will often dump large amounts of content that the coach has difficulty understanding. Understanding content should not be the goal of a coach, but understanding the meaning of that content for the individual is.

CASE STUDY

Rob has asked to talk about a promotion interview he has just failed. He starts to describe in detail the questions and the answers he gave. Since Rob is in a highly technical role, the questions and his answers are unintelligible to the listener, unless Rob is asked to explain them in simpler and simpler terms. This would help the listener understand content, but it would serve little purpose for Rob.

The listener holds back from asking for clarification as the content washes over them, until Rob puts in the throw-away line, 'I've now completely messed up my career here'. The listener recognizes that this comment is central to understanding his purpose in having the conversation, and says, 'Messed up your career. That's a strong phrase.

Help me understand what you mean by messed up your career?'. The request for clarification helps Rob to think more deeply about what he means, so his thinking moves forward.

Summarizing

Summarizing is feeding back to the other person what they have understood so far. Summarizing what another person has said is particularly helpful in the setting up stage of a conversation. This is because the invitation to talk about something that has been fermenting inside the head often means that, when it is first articulated, it comes out in a jumble of ideas and a stream of consciousness. In this spilling out, the speaker often loses track of what they have said, so intent are they on getting it out.

The purpose of summarizing is to hold up a mirror so that the speaker can look at what they have said and decide which threads are most important for them in taking the conversation further.

CASE STUDY

John has had a poor performance review and now has to set some objectives for the next year. Given the opportunity to talk about setting objectives, he starts with a rush of thoughts about the unfairness of the appraisal process, the partiality of his boss, the number of conflicting demands on him, the challenges of a newly formed team and the bringing together of two departments. The coach summarizes that, so far, he has talked about his feelings about his review rating and his boss's role in that. He has also spoken about the heavy demands on his time, and the need to get a new team performing quickly. He has also touched on the demands of bringing together two very different departments into one whole. The coach checks out if he has been correctly understood, and when he confirms the accuracy of the summary, the coach asks him to identify which aspects it would be most useful to explore, given his purpose of wanting a more successful performance review next year. Put in that light, John then decides that key to this will be the successful merger of the departments. John now knows that he has been heard, but he has also been able to select the most useful route for taking the conversation forward.

Reflecting

Reflecting is the simple act of repeating back to the other person key words or phrases that they have used. This requires the active listening of the coach because the selection of the phrase is central. The reflection is of ideas, images or feelings that the coach hears are important to the central purpose of the conversation. The repeating of a phrase or word, when well chosen, acts as a prompt to further thought, particularly if it is offered in a tone that suggests the listener's interest and curiosity. The speaker, caught up in their own thoughts, may not realize what they have said until the coach shows it back to them. A thought that has only previously existed in their head takes on a new life when it is expressed back to them by another person.

CASE STUDY

Gwyneth had taken a career break after having her second child and was promoted soon after her return. She appeared to be coping well and to be dealing with the demands of home and work comfortably. She asked for a coach to help her with some of the new business aspects of the role. When she met with the coach, she spoke clearly about the demands of the new role, and an agenda around helping her to develop a more strategic approach was developing. She then dropped in the phrase 'sometimes I think people believe I just got lucky in getting this job on returning from my career break'. The coach repeated the phrase 'just got lucky'. Gwyneth picked up the reflection and opened up into owning her own feelings that she had got lucky and that somehow she did not deserve it, particularly when she had days when she would rather be at home with her young children. Had the coach challenged Gwyneth by saying, 'Look at your track record there is nothing lucky about your promotion', the issue would have gone back underground. By reflecting it back to her, Gwyneth was able to talk about her own ambivalence about the role and the demands of wanting to be both a good manager and a good mother. She was then more able to define what her true purpose was in the coaching conversation – to find a way of doing her job without feeling guilty.

Empathizing

Empathizing is accepting that this is how it is for the speaker, even if it would not be experienced that way by the listener. It is the ability to understand how it is from the other person's position without having to take their point of view. It is an important listening skill in building connection because it signals to the other person that their position makes sense from where they are standing.

It does not mean that you have to share that viewpoint. As the Manager Coach you may know very well why they were not chosen to head up that project, indeed you may have made the decision. However, if they are to move on they need to be freed from having to defend themselves. Sympathy, offered from the best of intents, can work to hold the person in the same place.

CASE STUDY

Jane had worked for many years as a secretary for one boss. She prided herself on her commitment to doing her best for that person. When cutbacks meant she was having to support three other managers, she was deeply hurt. She saw it as an affront to the loyalty she had always shown. Other secretaries supported her in her feelings of hurt through telling her how awful it must be for her that she had been discounted, and they encouraged her to dig her heels in and refuse to take on the extra work. In their well-intentioned sympathy, their unintended outcome was that Jane's view of herself became less and less confident. She saw herself as a victim and her feelings of powerlessness increased. The Personnel Manager decided to approach the issue with her, and after listening to her said empathically, 'If I were in your shoes, I would feel the way you do. It can't be easy having to change the way you work when you have liked the way things have been'. She did not pretend that things could go back, but in acknowledging that Jane's position was a valid one, she was also signalling that she saw Jane as an adult rather than a helpless child. They were then able to look at what Jane valued most in her role, and how elements of that could be built into the new arrangement.

Being able to apply Type A listening is a bedrock of building the coaching conversation. It allows the content to be laid out and for the process of discriminating amongst the content to find what is helpful to be identified. It is a necessary part of coaching, but it is not enough.

CASE STUDY

Ben was an administrator in his 30s who said he was frustrated in his role and was keen to move into something more challenging. His boss suggested he talk with an internal coach as he was unsure how to help Ben, since he could not see any obvious openings. The coach, listening at content level, saw the issue as one of clarifying his skills, putting together a c.v., giving him some help in interview skills and encouraging him to network in other departments. What the coach did not hear were Ben's explanations as to why he had failed to do anything about his job situation except to moan. The coach did not hear the commonalities in the stories he told about his career, which were linked by the belief that he had been let down by a series of previous bosses. The coach did not hear the beliefs Ben held that, as a man without a degree about to hit his 40s, he could not expect more than what he had. What Ben was telling the coach in the level beneath content was that he lacked any confidence that his situation could change. Because the coach failed to listen closely to what was in the subglacial zone, the issues were never discussed and the coach became increasingly frustrated with Ben's failure to act on actions they had agreed.

The failure of Ben's case was not that the coach failed to listen, it is that they listened at the wrong level. The coach listened and responded to the content of what Ben was saying, when what they needed to do was to look for the meaning in what Ben was saying. Listening for meaning requires a different set of skills. That listening starts with being able to stop listening to ourselves.

The concern of most people when they are asked to coach another is that they will not know what to ask. Having accepted that coaching is not about offering wisdom in the form of advice, they switch their attention to asking questions, and become caught up in trying to think of good and clever questions. All the time the other person is speaking, their self-conscious self is desperately thinking 'What do I ask next?'. They are caught up in worrying that they will lose face if they don't have a question immediately on their lips the moment the other stops speaking. The focus on themselves stops them from fully listening, and makes it difficult to stay engaged. Letting go of worrying about what to ask next is the key to starting to fully listen. Accepting that message is difficult, but two things help:

1. The human brain works six times quicker than the human mouth. This means that the brain will do the work for you if you let it. Focusing your energy on an internal dialogue about what you should or should not be asking, combined with an internal critic who is looking at how you are performing, are two ways of ensuring interference to what the brain should be doing – focusing on the other person.

2. Letting go of worrying about questions and listening to all the information that the other person is leaking to you guarantees that questions emerge without having to be worked on.

These other forms of information are available to us when we use Type B listening skills.

Type B listening

Type B listening is listening below the water level. It is focused on understanding what extra information the other person holds that could be helpful to the conversation, which they may not articulate. Type B listening happens when we shift our attention from understanding content and look instead for evidence of:

- the energy the person is showing and how it changes as they talk
- the beliefs they hold about themselves
- the values they are displaying
- the emotion that surrounds the content of what they are saying
- the personality clues that are revealed in what they say
- the atmosphere that is present as they speak
- the information that their body is offering.

All of us are Type B listeners, it is simply that it gets driven underground by what we learn about organizational behaviour.

CASE STUDY

Oliver is a totally task-driven manager who is so intent on delivering goals that he pays little attention to social niceties. When he is told that he needs to show more empathy to his staff, he is perplexed. He claims he doesn't notice what is happening for other people, so he is genuinely surprised when he hears that they are demotivated or dissatisfied. His coach challenges him on his assertion that he does not notice what is happening with other people and asks him to identify anything he has noticed about the coach during the session. He says that he notices that they look more relaxed than in the previous session; that they have more energy and that they seem more interested in what he is saying. His observations were 100 per cent accurate and the coach congratulated him on his observational skills. He shrugged them aside 'Well, yes, but what do I do with that information?'.

Oliver's response was an honestly confused one. He noticed things but he did not know what to do with the information because he did not feel that it had any value. He knew how to feed back to staff that they had not delivered work to the standards he expected, but he did not know how to feed back that he noticed they seemed dejected by his feedback. His view was that using the observation was something that would slow down the process of getting the work done.

Oliver is not alone in seeing Type B listening as an interference to dealing with content, but he is wrong. When we are looking to help staff raise their performance Type B listening can be the shortcut to getting to the solution. The other great gift of Type B listening is that it does not require you to think of smart questions, it simply asks you to notice and to test out your observations.

CASE STUDY

Sonia was in the identified talent pool of a telecoms company. She had always delivered on tough challenges, but her motivation had collapsed following organizational changes. She was now being seen as under-performing and the organization offered her the chance to get back on track through some external coaching. The coaching quickly established that the conditions she needed to do her best work were no longer on offer and the issue became how and when to exit. She started to explore options and quickly came back with two possibilities. One had a strong link with her established skills and involved working in another large plc. The other was an opportunity to join a small organization where she could make a big impact but the risks were much higher. As a single parent, she did not know if she could take that risk. She spent the session going backwards and forwards in a SWOT analysis of the two possibilities. The coach said little as she practised the arguments for and against each case without prompting. The coach did not even listen that closely to the content, but she did observe. Finally, she commented, 'I notice every time you talk about the small start up your energy level goes up'. Sonia leapt at the observation in agreement. Very rapidly she made the decision that she would go for the more risky option. What the coach had offered her in the observation was permission to listen to the stronger voice within her, and to trust it. The SWOT analysis revealed her thinking self, but committing to a decision came from having her motivations reflected back to her, as reflected in the way her energy levels went up and down.

Listening for Type B information releases the coach from the need to be clever. It simply asks that you listen closely with all your senses and test out your observations. It does not even matter if your observations are wrong, because the other person will correct you.

Content	Listening Type A	Listening Type B	Possible Outcome
The team is not doing what I want of them	*Clarification:* What is it you want them to be doing?	*Emotion:* I think I hear some sadness in your voice as you say that	They agree with you and then talk about how they feel they are not leading the team *Or* They correct you – it's not sadness, it's frustration/disappointment/ exhaustion and they re-direct the conversation to whichever is most accurate
The meeting went really badly this morning, I would like to talk about what I did wrong	*Summary:* You think the meeting went badly because of how you behaved	*Beliefs:* I sense you believe you are responsible for how meetings go	The observation is correct and allows for a discussion of what they are or are not responsible for in meetings *Or* They challenge the idea of being responsible, which allows the coach to ask about what they do believe about themselves in meetings
My job share partner is letting me down by not pulling their weight	*Reflection:* Not pulling their weight. Say some more about that	*Body information:* As you said that, I noticed your body slumped down as though you are carrying the weight of the work	The observation encourages the other person to be open about what carrying a job share partner is like for them *Or* They feed back that that is how they normally sit, but they now know that the coach is focused on them, which will encourage more openness

Figure 5.3 Different interpretations depending on which type of listening you are using

I am finding it difficult to prioritize because everyone wants everything at the same time, and I find it hard to put people off	Empathy: If I was in your position I can see that prioritizing would be hard for me	Personality: I sense in what you say that you like to be seen as someone who does not let other people down	The observation is correct and allows them to talk about what is important to them about not letting people down Or The observation is challenged, 'Sometimes you have to let people down', and allows them to define more closely where they feel they can and cannot say 'No'
I have had it with this place. No one appreciates me	Reflection: Appreciation. What sort of appreciation is important to you?	Energy: You sound as though your energy has drained away	The comment allows them to focus on the effect on them of being drained of energy, before then identifying when they feel more energized Or They dismiss the idea of having energy drained away. It is suppressed anger they are feeling. The observation allows them to express anger, which until then they have been holding on to, and which blocks them from seeing anything of value happening to them at work

Figure 5.3 Continued

No one type of listening is better than the other. Type A listening used alone brings a quality to the discussion that is absent from most conversations at work. Type B listening asks that you take a risk – that you move beyond being the skilled content listener; that you forget about asking questions and give focused attention to the other person. By giving that focus you will know when a Type A intervention is appropriate, and when to bring in an observation from your Type B repertoire. Type B listening, used alone, would risk encouraging disclosure without a focus on outcome. Type A listening used alone can miss identifying what is really causing the difficulty, so that actions are agreed but not implemented. Put together, they provide the means of getting to meaningful outcomes quickly.

Selecting between which type of listening is most relevant at any moment asks that the Manager Coach is constantly asking themselves, 'What is my purpose in asking this question, or offering this feedback?'. The concept of purpose from the coach's perspective is different from that of the coachee. For a coach any intervention is made with the purpose of enabling the speaker to understand more clearly. For the coach, purpose provides a compass point for listening. How does the question serve the purpose of the conversation, as distinct from my own curiosity?

When I first began coaching, I was fortunate to work with a number of people who worked for well-known public figures. Fuelled by celebrity voyeurism I would find myself asking questions in order to feed my own curiosity, rather than in order to help their thinking. My questions were of no help to my coaching client since they already had plenty of information on their boss. It was only when I concentrated on client purpose that my focus in listening moved to where it needed to be.

EXERCISE 1

Before applying your Type B listening skills you need to recognize that you have them. The next time you are in a meeting where your input is not critical, use the time to listen to the Type B information you are receiving. Do this by focusing on one or two people in the room (the most vociferous and the quietest).

In Type B mode listen to what they reveal.

■ Changes in their body language as the meeting progresses.
■ Shifts in their energy levels and what this relates to in the content of the discussion.
■ Personality clues in the interventions they make.
■ Values that are shown by the way they interact with others.

Sense also the atmosphere in the room and any changes you note as the meeting progresses.

Afterwards check out with someone else in the room (someone you know well) how they think the meeting went. They will focus on the content, because they will assume that is what you would expect). Surprise them by sounding out with them some of your own Type B observations and see the effect. They will not necessarily have noticed the same things as you, but you can be sure they will have done some Type B listening.

Discuss with them what could have been different if some of that Type B listening had been brought into the room.

EXERCISE 2

Once you are confident that you are a Type B listener then experiment with slipping a Type B comment into a work conversation, and notice what happens. Does the conversation move in a different way as a result of your observation? Does the individual use it to agree and build on your feedback? Do they disagree and correct?

Summary

This has been a long chapter because the Set Up stage of a coaching conversation is the most important. If you get the foundations right, then the rest of the conversation flows more easily. In order to get those foundations right you need to:

- Observe rather than scan your staff so that you can identify a coaching opportunity.
- Establish the purpose of the conversation without putting pressure on the premature identification of goals.
- Be comfortable with the purpose.
- Listen with intent through using the core Type A skills of attention, clarification, reflection, summarizing and empathy.
- Listen with intent through using the added-value Type B skills of listening for body information, energy, emotion, personality, values and beliefs.
- Move between the two modes of listening in response to what is appropriate to the purpose of the conversation.

References

1. Whitmore, J. (2002) *Coaching for Performance.* Nicholas Brearley.
2. Greene, J. and Grant, A.B. (2003) *Solution-Focused Coaching.* Pearson Education.

3. Ibarra, H. (2004) *Working Identity.* Harvard Business School Press.

4. Locke, E. (1999) Motivation through conscious goal setting. *Applied and Preventative Psychology*, 5 (2), 117–24.

5. Hammond, S.A. and Mayfield, A.B. (2004) *The Thin Book of Naming Elephants.* Thin Book Publishing.

6. Covey, S. (2004) *The 7 Habits of Highly Effective People.* Free Press.

7. O'Connor, J. (2001) *NLP Workbook.* Element.

6

Tangibles

Reality is only seen when the mirror is clear.
Anonymous

In giving time to the Set Up phase of the conversation, the coach is showing that they are offering support for the other's thoughts, and that the agenda is in their hands. In moving the conversation forward the coach continues to show that support, but they have to do more if the other person is to be helped to change. The coach needs to enable them to examine their situation and the tangibles they have attached to it. In this way, they are able to discover if there are other tangibles they have overlooked in their telling of their story. In Einstein's words, 'Reality is merely an illusion, although a very persistent one'. The Manager Coach offers the opportunity to discover alternative realities.

This means moving from the rapport-building listener to the listener whose purpose is to wipe the steam off the mirror, so that the other person can see themselves and their situation more clearly. When a member of staff tells of a difficulty they are facing, they will have told the story to themselves many times. It will have been crafted into a final version that is crystallized in their mind. The task of the coach is to unfreeze that version so that they have the opportunity to look at it from another perspective, and in so doing be able to find a viewpoint from which solutions can emerge.

The skill base of the coach now has to expand, accessing abilities to challenge the other's thoughts, because in so doing they will make available to the other person more information than they currently hold.

Getting specific

The first challenge a solution focused coach can offer is to force attention on to the specific. People are comfortable in a world of generalities. It allows for easy labelling:

- 'It's awful around here.'
- 'It's impossible to deliver that outcome.'

- 'I'm useless at ...'
- 'It will never happen.'

The companion of easy labelling is the easy get out:

- If 'it's awful around here' – it's their fault.
- If 'it's impossible to deliver that outcome' – there is no point trying.
- If 'I am useless at ...' – it will never get any better.
- If 'it will never happen' – I don't need to do anything differently.

Unfreezing those positions means inviting the other person to tighten up their thinking through asking them to be specific.

SAMPLE DIALOGUE

Coachee: It's awful around here.

Manager Coach: What *specifically* is awful around here? (*Manager does not allow the generality to pass unnoticed*).

Coachee: Morale – everyone feels that there is no point trying to reach our targets when it doesn't make any real difference to our pay.

Manager Coach: You used the word everyone, but I am interested in *what specifically* is affecting your morale. (*Manager refuses to let the coach hide behind the cloak of everyone*).

Coachee: The sense that no matter how hard I work no one notices my efforts and only notices the things that go wrong.

Manager Coach: You said no one notices – *who specifically* are you thinking of when you say that? (*Again, Manager hears the generality and challenges it*).

Coachee: I suppose I mean you.

Manager Coach: So now I understand. You feel that I am not appreciating your efforts and only give time to picking up what's not OK. (*Manager states openly what the coachee has been unable to express*).

Coachee:	Does that sound awful? (*Coachee feels uncomfortable at this exposure and looks for reassurance*).
Manager Coach:	It sounds like you are feeling resentful, so *what specifically* would you like to be different from now on? (*Manager does not get hooked by the coachee's request for reassurance, and keeps them focused on taking responsibility for what they want to be different*).

The Manager Coach and their direct report now have a workable agenda: to look at how they can work together so that the staff member is more motivated. The coachee has also been given responsibility for shaping the outcome.

Individuals become wedded to a story that offers no possibility of change, and want to play it out again and again. Change starts from challenging them to look at their narrative with a sharper focus.

CASE STUDY

Grant heads up an IT team in an organization in the finance sector. The team has been enlarged because of a high-visibility project that requires additional resources which have been drafted in from other departments. The process of assimilation is proving difficult because the pressure of delivering on the project is not allowing for an easy transition. In particular, the original team members are feeling that their turf is being taken over by these newcomers. One after the other they trail through Grant's office moaning about how awful life is. At the end of his tether as another knock comes on the door, he intervenes before they start. 'If you are coming to tell me how difficult things are for you right now, I am happy to listen, provided that you tell me what specifically you want to be different, and how you think we can do it'.

The staff member looks askance at this intervention. This had not been the tangible they wanted to present. In posing the challenge, Grant is offering them the opportunity to make a difference if they will accept it. If they do accept, then a FAST coaching opportunity has been set up.

The fascination of the problem

The one certainty when a coaching conversation begins is that the coachee is holding a problem. The problem can be a familiar friend that has lived with them for many years. For staff who have gone through development courses, the problem will have a short-hand description:

- 'I am unassertive.'
- 'I am a Thinker not a Feeler.'
- 'I am an Introvert.'
- 'I am a Monitor Evaluator.'
- 'I get people to do things through reward and punishment.'

The obvious approach to a problem is to try and understand the cause.

- Why are you unassertive?
- Why do you believe thinking is the only way to approach issues?
- Why are you introverted?
- Why do you evaluate what everyone says?
- Why do you think rewards and punishments are the only things that motivate performance?

Understand the cause, and the logic argues that the action to be taken will emerge. It's the approach of organizational analysis. Understand why a product isn't selling to its intended target group and a successful new strategy can be developed. Understand why a merger failed to deliver and the problem will not recur with a future merger. The fascination with problems is the meat and drink of organizational life. As individuals we are equally fascinated by our own problems. It is why, when individuals are genuinely offered the opportunity to talk about themselves, they will speak with ease about their problem. Building rapport requires that the coach shows that they are comfortable with the other person talking about their problem.

Problem talk is logical, but it is not necessary. What Solution Focused therapists discovered through their interest in finding out what worked best in moving people forward within short timeframes, is that progress comes more quickly if problem talk is limited.[1] Helping the client comes not from understanding the problem better, but from helping them to see the problem from a different perspective, i.e. one that assumes that they have the resources to deal with the problem. The client often understands the cause of their difficulty very well but nothing changes in their behaviour. Or they are so comfortable talking about the problem that talking about it becomes their *raison d'être*.

In their work, Solution Focused therapists have found that moving the individual from a focus on the problem to the identification of possible solutions begins with avoidance of the question why?

Why?

'Why' is an instinctive question. It is the question that fascinates us as a child, both because of our curiosity and because we discover that it is a good way of holding adult attention. It is the question that is used hundreds of times every day in organizations, and for much of the time it is helpful. It is important to understand why a manufacturing process has failed, why a rail accident occurred or why staff resist health and safety procedures. It can be enlightening to understand why people behave in a certain way. However, within a FAST coaching conversation, which is focused on making progress, it is a deflection.

Consider the following problem focused conversation.

Manager: I have noticed you are still staying later than any of your team. I thought you were going to delegate more.

Coachee: I know I should but I am an unassertive sort of person. I hate asking other people to do things, particularly if it means they will have to stay late.

Manager: *Why* do you think you are unassertive with your staff, when I have heard you on the phone being very assertive with difficult customers.

Coachee: I don't know. I think it's because it matters to me that they like me.

Manager: *Why* does it matter to you so much?

Coachee: Because my work colleagues are the people I spend most time with. To me they are family.

> *Manager:* I can see you enjoy working with them but *why* are they so important to you?
>
> *Coachee:* Because I don't have a partner right now.

In a few well-meant interventions, the conversation has moved from an observation on a failure to delegate to a discussion of their personal life. The coachee is now even more aware of why it is difficult for them to be assertive, but no better equipped to deal with it. The manager assumed that if he could help the other person understand the root cause of their lack of assertion, appropriate actions would emerge. This could be true in a long-term psychoanalytic relationship, but this is not what the Manager Coach is offering.

The question 'why?', posed with an interrogatory voice, leaves the other person feeling they have to defend or explain themselves. For those people who genuinely don't know 'why', the question forces them to produce an explanation that they hope will be acceptable.

The question 'why?', acts as a magnifying glass to problems when what the Manager Coach needs is that the problem shrinks through finding a position from where solutions can emerge. The question also leaves the Manager Coach potentially holding information that they have no ability to deal with. A conversation that began as an offer to look at delegating better has moved to the point where the coach could, if they continued the 'why?' line of questioning, get themselves into a depth that is beyond their ability. Having opened up a line of enquiry the coachee will feel exposed if their manager suddenly switches direction, because they don't how to handle the underlying cause of their difficulty with assertion.

An alternative questioning route:

> *Manager:* I have noticed you are still staying later than any of your team. I thought we had agreed that you were going to delegate more.
>
> *Coachee:* I know I should, but I am an unassertive sort of person. I hate asking people to do things that means they have to stay late.
>
> *Manager:* I know it's difficult for you to ask other people to do things, but I also hear you being assertive with some of our difficult customers. *How do you do that? (Manager acknowledges the*

problem, but draws attention to another tangible – an area where the problem does not exist.)

Coachee: I hadn't really thought about that, but I suppose it's because I focus on balancing what is fair to the customer and what is fair to the organization. When I think the balance is wrong, I will stand up for the organization.

Manager: That seems a helpful way of allowing the assertive you to be used. How do you feel when you do that? *(Manager draws attention to the fact she is using the skill of assertiveness effectively.)*

Coachee: I feel fine when I know I have got a fair outcome and I have not been rude or disrespectful to the other person. That's important to me, because I hate to be disliked.

Manager: So knowing that you can be assertive providing that you focus on fairness and do it with respect, what would you like to do differently with your team? *(Manager offers her back the framework she uses in order to be assertive, as a means of her identifying her own solution.)*

Coachee: I would like to agree some ground rules about how we allocate work, so that it is fair to everyone including me.

Manager: What might those ground rules look like? *(Manager has helped her to focus on an outcome and shifted her attention away from the problem.)*

The staff member still holds a need to be liked by their staff. They are still without a partner. However, the Manager Coach has enabled them to see a link with resources they use in other situations and how application of those resources can be made to their present difficulty. By doing so a new tangible has been brought into their line of sight from which they can find a means of making progress. The manager did not focus on setting a goal of being assertive, he focused on finding a solution to one situation in which they were unassertive. In doing so he was following the 'pebble principle' – of throwing a stone that the other person can use to break the surface of a directly relevant issue, in the belief that through experiencing success the ripples will start to roll out. The next time they experience a situation that calls on them to assert themselves with staff, they will have available to them a resource they were not previously aware of.

The instinct to ask 'Why' is so strong that removing it from a coaching conversation takes practice.

NOT 'WHY' EXERCISE

Step One
Start by noticing how many times in a day you ask 'why?' and how many times others ask it of you. Notice your own response to the question. When is it helpful? When does it make you feel defensive?

Step Two
Having noticed how often you ask the question, start to experiment. When the word 'why' comes to your lips ask yourself: 'What is my purpose in asking the question, and is the question "why?" the best means for getting that purpose met?'.

Quantum questions

The questions a Manager Coach needs to use are quantum questions. Quantum questions are questions that help build towards outcomes and are different in their quality from the 'why?' question. They are quantum because they enable the transition from one energy state to another. They leverage the move from being stuck to being able to act.

The questions that have these qualities and are most likely to build towards outcomes are:

- What?
- How?
- When?
- Where?

Since these are also questions you ask every day – how are they different from 'why?'

The difference between 'why?' questions and quantum questions is the difference between standing on one spot and digging down, and getting into a helicopter in order to see what is on the whole terrain, before deciding where you want to plant.

Quantum questions invite the person to find different tangibles from the ones they have become attached to. They are questions that enable the problem-holder to shift their perspective, so that they can see possibility rather than failure.

What?

Your staff member tells you that a project is going hay-wire. Rather than ask 'why?', which will allow them to unburden on how unreasonable the assignment is and their own feelings of failure, you ask 'what?' (See Figure 6.1.)

Underpinning every 'what?' question is the coach's determination to help the other person unearth data that will help them move from their present situation of being stuck. 'What?' questions are quantum questions because they focus attention on moving forward.

What else?

There is another 'What?' question that is invaluable to the Manager Coach. The question, 'What else?'.

It is invaluable because it encourages the other person to go further in their thinking, through your encouragement. While the question 'Anything else?' may have the same intent, it can be read as a signal of the listener's desire to bring things to an end. 'What else?' suggests that the other person has more to say that will be relevant. To the questioner's mind, asking the question several times will sound repetitive. However, for the speaker, the question allows them to look inside for longer, and they will not notice the repetition until they have exhausted their thinking. The purpose in asking the question several times is not to encourage a litany of complaints, but to generate the most relevant information for defining the focus of attention.

There is now a clear understanding by both parties of what is the best use of time and what the Manager Coach can bring to the conversation. Without the 'what else?', expediency leads us to work on what is first presented. The Manager Coach could have spent the time mapping out the organizational structure and the job roles as he saw them (if he had that knowledge). Alternately, he could have swiftly advised the coachee to talk with HR. Without taking time to understand the real need, both these approaches would have been ineffective.

Question	Purpose
What is happening right now?	To collect evidence on how the problem is showing itself
What are you most worried about?	Within this big picture of anxiety, what is it really important to pay attention to?
What do you need to do right now?	Separate out what can be done now from the totality of the issue
What would be a sign that things are improving?	To heighten their awareness of any signals of improvement so that they recognise rather than dismiss them
What help do you need to get things back on track?	To establish specifics that could make a difference
What do you need to do differently?	To focus their attention on their own agency and to identify specifics that would make a difference
What have you learnt from this that you can use?	To remind them that they are learning in the process of doing and that learning can be applied
What decisions do you have to make?	To separate what has to be addressed now and what has lower urgency
What is the most important thing for you to change?	To understand which part of the whole has most meaning for them in terms of the attention it deserves
What are the risks in this?	To establish the size and importance of the risks
What do you want to do to manage them?	To affirm that they can take some control of those risks

Figure 6.1 'What' questions

SAMPLE DIALOGUE

Coachee: I don't know how anyone gets to move around in this business. I need some information.

Manager Coach: OK, you have a need for information on how to change roles. What else?

Coachee: Even if I knew there was a system, I wouldn't know if I have the sort of skills that are needed in other parts of the business.

Manager Coach: So you are not sure of the skills needed elsewhere. What else?

Coachee: I am not really sure how I am doing right now, so would anyone else want me?

Manager Coach: You are unsure how your performance is being seen, so it is difficult to judge whether you should make an application right now. What else?

Coachee: I think that is it.

Manager Coach: Thanks for that. You have told me about your lack of information on jobs, your lack of knowledge on the skills needed in other areas, and your lack of any sense of how well you are doing. Which of these is most important to you?

Coachee: It has to be knowing how I am doing, so I can get a feel of where I need to develop if I am to move on from here.

Manager Coach: Good, that helps me to see that you need to look at your performance and any development gaps. To do that can you tell me how you see things, and what specifically you want feedback on, so I can offer you some?

Coachee: Yes – that's exactly what I want.

How?

Your staff member tells you that their team is dysfunctional because of personality clashes within it.

Rather than exploring 'why?' it is dysfunctional, which will put the magnifying glass on their failure to manage personality clashes, you ask 'how' questions (See Figure 6.2.)

The 'how?' question draws attention to how large the issue is. When we are focused on a difficulty, we develop blurred vision on size and we inflate impact. 'How?' questions about frequency and impact allow for resizing and, in doing so, allow in another perspective. A team that is dysfunctional 20 per cent of the time is working well for 80 per cent of the time. Establishing the 80 per cent allows for looking at what is happening during the time when the problem is not present. A problem focus sees only what is happening when the problem is there.

The 'how?' question can also be used to help the coachee recognize what they are doing that contributes to the problem not being there. The Manager Coach could ask, 'How do you contribute to the team's poor working together?'. This may be a covert way of asking 'Why are you failing as a manager?'. A more

Question	Purpose
How do personality clashes get in the way of the team being effective?	To establish specifics against the context of performance delivery
How often do the personality clashes get in the way of doing good work?	To establish the size of the problem
How would you like it to be different?	To understand the change they are looking for
How have you still managed to deliver with such a dysfunctional team?	To draw attention to what they can do as distinct from their awareness of what they can't
How can you use those skills to address what is happening right now?	To help make connections between resources that have been used in previous situations and a current need
How would you know that things were improving?	To encourage them to identify signs of progress
How can you make more use of what is working OK in the team?	To show that doing more of what works is as important as focusing on what needs to be done differently

Figure 6.2   'How' questions

useful approach is to help the other person see what they contribute when the team is working better, through asking, 'How have you managed to keep this team performing most of the time?'. This enables the coachee to identify behaviours that are helpful to the team, and to then consider how they could be applied to the current difficulty. 'How?' questions are quantum questions because they discover resources available to bring about the change.

There is one other 'how?' question that is useful to the coach. The question: 'How do you know that?'.

How do you know that?

This is a valuable question because it both provides challenge and can be used to draw attention to resources.

CASE STUDY

Clare was a difficult and demanding coachee who had a high investment in showing that her situation could never change. Week after week her coach tried to help her find a new job that matched with her considerable abilities. Week after week, Clare would dismiss the opportunities as not worthy of her. Asking the question 'why?' nothing was good enough for her, led into a discussion of the underlying feelings of defensiveness she had as a result of being ousted from a high-profile job. It also touched on even deeper-seated issues about her identity. Being a highly protected person, she quickly dismissed the issue of her own feelings of failure as no longer relevant, because the causative event had happened some while ago. Fuelled by desperation as Clare critiqued yet another opportunity that had come to her from a head-hunter, her coach simply asked 'How do you know that the job is not good enough for you?'. Clare started on a list of possible reasons and then halted saying, 'You are right, I don't know, I just assume'. That recognition allowed her to draw up her list of assumptions and to check them out with the head-hunter. In the process her assumptions proved faulty and her motivation to apply for the job increased. When she was appointed to the job, she had forgotten the reservations she once had, and she moved into the role with enormous energy. Without that 'how?' question it would never have happened.

'How?' is also valuable because it encourages people to touch on their resources by asking a question that invites a recognition of their capability.

> CASE STUDY
>
> James was struggling with his supervisor who was very different from him in personality. James was a high-energy, outspoken individual, his supervisor, Calum, was much quieter. New to supervision, he lacked confidence in dealing with staff who were older than himself. When James moaned yet again about how his ideas never got a hearing with Calum, his coach asked him to explain 'How he knew that his ideas would not get past Calum'. James told the coach in a voice of resignation, that whenever he went into Calum's office and Calum had his head down, focused on something, he knew that he would fail. He knew, too, because whenever he brought up something new in a meeting Calum would not respond. The coach fed back to James that he already knew things that would help him make more impact on Calum. He had identified that Calum could only focus on one thing at a time, and he had identified that throwing new things at him did not lead to a response. Asking James how he could use what he knew to get better results, enabled him to adopt a new approach. He asked for time with Calum, rather than arriving unexpectedly. He only offered one idea at a time, and he did not ask for an immediate response. The surprise for James was that using what he knew to look for a solution, rather than using what he knew as a reason for blame, so quickly led to results.

When?

A staff member comes in complaining that they are bored with their job and want a change. Rather than asking 'why?' the Manager Coach asks 'when?' (See Figure 6.3).

In asking the 'when?' question, the Manager Coach wrong-foots the other person. They are diverted from thinking about what they don't like by being

Question	Purpose
When do you feel more engaged in your work?	Provide information on what they like doing, in order to look for opportunities to build more in
When did you last feel challenged?	Help understanding of what challenge looks like to them and how frequently it occurs

Figure 6.3 'When' questions

challenged to recognize that their dissatisfaction is coming from not having enough of what they do like. A new tangible comes into their frame of reference. Through asking the 'when?' question the Manager Coach is able to help draw up a picture of what job satisfaction looks like, so that either more of it can be built into their role, or they can start looking with more purpose for their next role. This can then be followed up by further 'when?' questions (Figure 6.4).

Question	Purpose
When will you know that your job is becoming more satisfying again?	To increase sensitivity to the signs of change
When are you going to start working on redefining your priorities in line with our discussion?	To test out their commitment
When is your deadline for knowing whether your job can be made more workable?	To provide an outcome focus so that the issue does not drift

Figure 6.4 More 'when' questions

The power of the 'when?' question as a quantum question is that it encourages the coachee to do two things:

1. to identify evidence of the desired change
2. to build a sense of commitment towards doing something differently.

CASE STUDY

Andrew was a brand manager with a fast-moving consumer goods (FMCG) organization who came for coaching because he was dissatisfied with his role. He was highly ambitious and spent much of the first session telling the coach how able he was and what he expected from the company. The fact that he had come to an external coach demonstrated that at some level he recognized that his employer did not share his self-assessment, since the opportunities he claimed he should have were not being offered to him. In order to cut across this problem talk masquerading as self-justification, the coach asked, 'When did you feel that your abilities were being fully utilized?'. Andrew then spoke with passion about an exercise where he and an external consultant had worked together to define a new strategy for a failing food product. The follow up question of, 'How long did it take to develop the idea for the strategy?', prompted the answer 'Half a day'. In minutes Andrew recognized the cause of his dissatisfaction. He was excited by the strategic exercise and judged himself by his ability to think creatively. In his current role he was judged by his ability to deliver the outcome of others' creativity over time, which held far less appeal for him. Recognizing this, he was then able to free up from anger with the company to look at where there was a market for the skills by which he wanted to be judged.

'When?' is recognized as a good question at the action-planning stage of a discussion as a means of encouraging commitment to act, but it is equally helpful in discovering the cause of procrastination.

CASE STUDY

Jacqueline knew exactly what she wanted to do. She wanted to go back to college to get an MBA. She even knew what she wanted to do with the qualification: a significant job in marketing with an international company working in fashion retail. She had a background that prepared her well and she had taken months investigating which MBA would suit her best. When she discussed it with her coach, there was always just one more piece of information she needed before making her decision. She presented herself as a highly analytical, professional woman with strong ambitions. After listening to her explain yet again how she needed more information before she could commit, her coach asked, 'When will you know that it is time to commit?'. At first Jacqueline prevaricated, before answering, 'When my mother tells me she supports me, and isn't disappointed that I am not married'.

All the time that Jacqueline had been presenting herself as a rational investigator, she had been avoiding the thing that was really stopping her committing to an MBA, her fear of her mother's disapproval. Once the issue became tangible, the coach was able to separate out two threads that had become entangled in Jacqueline's mind. Completing a MBA did not bring with it a guarantee of spinsterhood, any more than not doing an MBA guaranteed finding the perfect partner.

Once the threads were disentangled, her coach was able to talk with her about how she could discuss the issue of further study with her mother. She was then able to answer questions such as 'What do you want to say to your mother?', 'How do you need to prepare for that discussion?', and 'When will you do it?'.

Where?

Your staff member claims that it is impossible to prioritize because they are so overwhelmed with demands. Rather than asking 'why?' they can't prioritize, you ask 'where?' (See Figure 6.5).

'Where?' is a great quantum question because it throws focus on where making an effort will have a return. It looks to break down a generic label into parts that can be addressed. It also allows for drawing attention to underlying beliefs that are acting to limit freedom of choice.

Question	Purpose
Where does the workload feel most manageable?	To identify what is not a problem
Where would it be easiest for you to begin prioritizing?	What can be started on most easily
Where can you find some time to stand back and start making some decisions?	To find some space from which they can begin to identify what can be different
Where will you let go of work most easily?	To find what is not going to be difficult
Where is it written that you have to do everything?	To find what they are doing that they have no need or responsibility to be doing
Where is the greatest return on your effort?	To establish what is most worthwhile their giving time to
Where do you want to direct your efforts if you can make progress on prioritizing?	To find a motivator for doing things differently
Where will it be visibly different if you manage your priorities better?	To understand how they and others will know that things have changed

Figure 6.5 'Where' questions

CASE STUDY

Emma was a highly responsible analyst in a policy organization. Her role brought her into contact with some very senior public figures. She had a reputation for acting inappropriately because she would challenge individuals regardless of their seniority, if she believed their views were in opposition to those of her own organization. Given her relative junior status, this behaviour did not win her the recognition she thought her inputs deserved. She was seen as difficult, and a CEO had asked that she not be included in any future meetings. When Emma discussed the issue it was clear that, from her perspective, her inputs were driven by a strong commitment to her employer. In her presentation of the story she was the lone hero fighting for justice. The question 'Who else attends the meetings with you?', revealed that she was always one of a team. The question her coach then posed, 'Where is it written that you are solely responsible for the outcome of any meeting you attend?', allowed her to look at what she was and was not responsible for when she was involved in external meetings. It allowed her to set realistic objectives for her influence within a meeting, and to let go of the burden that if an outcome was not achieved she bore the responsibility.

In establishing a 360-degree view on tangibles from which solutions emerge, as distinct from the tangibles that the coachee already recognizes, quantum questions are one of the most powerful tools at a Manager Coach's disposal.

Quantum questions are open questions, but they are more than this. They are questions asked by a questioner who is always keeping their purpose in mind. They use them to raise the speaker into a helicopter from where they can look at their story with a perspective that was previously not available to them.

EXERCISE

As a Manager Coach you will want to build a databank of quantum questions. Questions that you know are helpful in getting a fuller picture of reality.

As a new coach you will find it helpful to keep a sheet with the headings:

- What?
- When?
- Where?
- How?

You may want to also add the injunction '*Don't ask why?*', as a reminder to you to apply this discipline when establishing the tangibles with your coachee.

As you start asking quantum questions make a list of those that hit the button and help move the conversation forward in a way that a 'why?' question could not.

You can test this out further by asking your coachee, as part of the review of the session, to tell you any questions that were helpful to their thinking. Coachees will not remember most of the questions you posed, but they will recall the ones that really shifted their view of the situation and themselves.

Sizing the problem

Every FAST coaching conversation is built on quantum questions, but sometimes you need more information before you are satisfied that the tangibles have been identified. This is where it can be helpful to size the problem.

Your staff member delivers a torrent of information relating to an issue that is impacting on their performance. As you listen it becomes difficult to separate out the issues, and to know where to begin. A shortcut route is to ask them to physically draw the problem and those things that are impacting on it as a series of circles, and to consider how large or small each circle should be.

EXAMPLE
Sally is about to go on maternity leave just as a series of initiatives she has been involved in are coming together. She has a team in which she has a strong role as the nurturing mother, and she is concerned that they will not perform to the same level if she is not there to drive their delivery. While she knows it is irrational, she hates the thought of someone standing in for her while she is away, and perhaps changing things that she had planned to do herself.

The presenting issue is sustaining performance while she is away. Affecting team performance are a number of issues, which Sally then places within the circle.

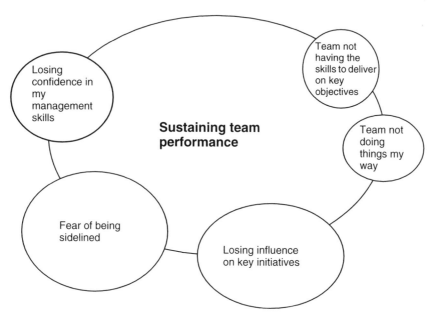

Figure 6.6 Sally's interpretation of the issue

Visualized in this way, Sally is able to recognize that it is herself, rather than the skills of her team, that is her main concern, and her Manager Coach can work with her on planning for going on maternity leave and managing the transition back.

CASE STUDY
Ray had been offered a job by a friend. It offered the possibility of great earnings in the longer term, but it also would mean a total commitment at a time when he was about to become a father. He was excited by the job offer, but said he could not take it because his wife would not want him to take on more responsibilities at this time. He was also not sure if he had the best match of skills for the role, and was concerned at letting his friend down. After to-ing and fro-ing between the various options, his coach asked him to map out the issue as a series of circles, whose size represented their importance in his mind.

Ray interpreted the exercise in his own way and represented the circles as seen in Figure 6.7.

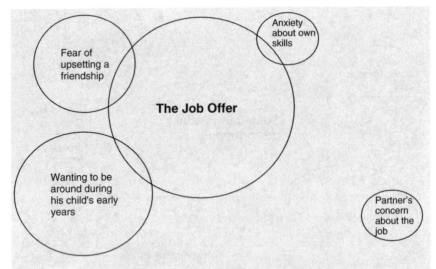

Figure 6.7 Ray's interpretation of the issue

When he looked at the issue visually it became clear to him that his partner was not putting any pressure on him. She was happy to go along with whatever he decided. However, he had a real anxiety about not being there at an important new stage in his life and it was this, rather than the skills issue, that was holding him back from agreeing. He was able to use the information to define how the job would need to be if he was to be able to commit to it, and to then discuss it with his friend. Expressing it openly allowed his friend to share his concerns that the timing of the job was not right for Ray. They were able to agree that he should not take on the job at this time, but that he would offer some paid consultancy on areas where he had particular skills. Their friendship remained intact and Ray felt better for having acknowledged his own feelings rather than deflecting them as being those of his partner.

Sizing the problem is a useful tool for working with individuals who are getting lost in multiple aspects impacting on an issue.

For visual thinkers, being asked to draw something can be more comfortable than continuing to talk about it. They enjoy the process of getting the sizes right, and it provides a shortcut in their thinking.

For auditory thinkers, who will talk long and fluently about an issue, cutting across their usual pattern by asking them to stop talking and draw will challenge them. However, it often provides the rapid clarity that their words are not providing.

<small>EXERCISE</small>

Experiment for yourself. Identify an issue that is currently unresolved because you have multiple perspectives on it. It could be work-related, or it could relate to your home life, e.g. deciding where to go on holiday, deciding whether to spend more money on your home or to move.

Identify the perspectives that are crowding into the issue and preventing you from committing to a decision. These could be factual or emotional. Draw them out according to the size of importance they have in your mind, as they relate to the decision.

Reflect on whether drawing them out in this way puts a different perspective on the issue and what you need to focus on in getting the decision right.

Making tangible through metaphors

Metaphors are liberally sprinkled across our daily interactions at work. We use them to draw comparisons between ourselves and our situation and another object, as a short-hand for describing our experience and feelings:

- It's like wading through treacle trying to get a decision made here.
- I've got a heart of stone when people start giving me excuses about deadlines.
- I am a leopard who can't change their spots.
- If we are going to have any chance of success against the competition, we have got to find a way of levelling the playing field.
- When she asked if she could join our project team, I asked her 'What she brought to this party?'.
- I feel like I am being stabbed in the back.
- Let's get all the ducks in a row on this one.
- I was 'in the zone' at the presentation.
- She thinks she can pull my strings.

Metaphors are used so liberally that we don't listen to the meaning behind the words. We assume we know what is meant. However, when we are in

Manager Coach mode and are listening to help get a fuller picture of the tangibles, metaphors provide powerful clues when we ally them to our quantum questions.

CASE STUDY

Ted is a long-serving manager who has an enormous sense of responsibility to his staff. He has taken over a department at a time of restructuring that has resulted in significant changes for many of the staff. He feels that his staff are not being properly supported by the organization and he spends a lot of time listening to their worries, whilst feeling powerless to do anything. He is single, without family responsibilities and it is clear to his coach that he is taking his worries home. He has lost weight, and he does not look well. When his coach feeds back to him how stressed he looks, he admits that he is not sleeping and is using his weekends as recovery time. When challenged on the degree of personal responsibility he is assuming, when there are direct reports who have a line responsibility for many of his staff, he dismisses the suggestion by saying. 'I know what I should do, but I am a good soldier'. The phrase leaps out at the coach, and they ask, 'What kind of good soldier?'. He then describes it as someone who never leaves his post, and does whatever is asked of him. Follow up questions of 'What else?', allow him to flesh out the picture. A good soldier, who wants the approval of his Senior Officers, and does not challenge orders. A soldier, who puts his troops before himself.

All of this described what Ted was doing in his role. Allowing him to expand on the metaphor then provided more data that could be examined with him, through testing out what was helpful and unhelpful in being a good soldier, and whether there were other ways of being a good soldier that he had not allowed himself.

Metaphors are gifts for Type B listening. Once they are heard in a coaching conversation, they can be focused on through asking the question:

'What kind of?'

The exploration can then be taken further through asking 'What else?', so that the full meaning the individual attaches to that metaphor can be made public.

EXAMPLE

Joan has been talking through a difficult relationship she has with a colleague, and announces that she has had enough of going over past history with her colleague, and has decided to *draw a line in the sand*. In Manager Coach mode he asks 'What kind of a line in the sand is that?'. Joan replies, 'It's a line that won't wash away easily because it is backed up with rocks'. Her Manager Coach asks 'What else?'. She replies, 'It's a line that has been made by a piece of weathered driftwood'. Her Manager Coach asks again 'What kind of driftwood'. Joan replies, 'The kind that has been around a while, and can survive storms'.

Her Manager Coach, in that brief exploration of the metaphor, now knows that Joan is committed to making a break with the past in terms of her relationship with her colleague. It is more than a form of words, it is based on a sense that in making the decision to draw that line she is drawing on strength.

Had the conversation gone differently, it would have identified a different need.

EXAMPLE

Joan has been talking through a difficult relationship she has with a colleague, and announces that has had enough of going over past history with her colleague and that she has decided to *draw a line in the sand*. In Manager Coach mode he asks, 'What kind of a line in the sand is that?'. Joan replies, 'It's a line that gets washed away every time the tide comes in'. The Manager Coach asks 'What else?'. She replies, 'It's on sand that is wet and slippery'. He asks again, What kind of wet and slippery sand?'. She replies, 'The sort that could pull you under'.

In that exploration of the metaphor, the Manager Coach now knows that Joan has little confidence that the line will hold, and fears that she will get pulled under. If the line is to hold, she has signalled that she needs help in how to hold it when she is put under pressure by the other person.

Metaphors are valuable for coaches,[2] because the choice of metaphor is never casual. It is chosen for its fit with how that person is experiencing themselves in that moment. By inviting them to expand on the metaphor through quantum questioning, you are enabling them to more fully recognize the power and meaning of the metaphor they have chosen. You help them to make more tangible the meaning that drove the selection of that metaphor.

EXERCISE

Stop for a moment and consider a metaphor that captures how you are experiencing life at the moment. This could be inside or outside of work.

Don't think too long, but use the first metaphor that comes to your mind.

Having identified the metaphor, ask yourself the question 'What kind of?' and list the thoughts that come to mind. If you find that one metaphor leads into identifying another, then follow the trail through more, 'What kind of . . .?' questions. Encourage yourself to explore more fully through asking yourself the 'What else?' question. When you have finished your line of thought, look at what you have revealed to yourself in the process of exploring the metaphor. What in it is useful to you?

If you can get a partner to do this with you, so relieving you of the necessity to ask yourself the questions, it will be even more valuable.

Summary

This chapter has focused on helping you build on the Set Up stage through helping the other person recognize information that is relevant to their issue and that is not available to them when they are considering the issue inside their own head.

The skills of clearing the mirror so that they can see the picture more clearly come from:

- Avoiding the question Why?.
- Asking the quantum questions of What, When, Where and How?.
- Asking questions that are driven by the Manager Coach's clarity of purpose.
- Enabling the coachee to size the problem accurately.
- Using metaphors to understand what is underneath the short-hand.

References

1. de Shazer, S. (1985) *Keys to Solutions in Brief Therapy*. Norton.
2. Lawley, J. and Tompkins, P. (2003) *Metaphors in Mind: Transforming Through Symbolic Modelling*. The Developing Company Press.

7

Assumptions

The least questioned assumptions are often the most questionable.

Paul Broca

God grant me the serenity to accept the things I cannot change, the courage to change the things I can and the wisdom to know the difference.

Reinhold Niebuhr

Exploring tangibles gives a wide-angle lens to someone who previously has had only a close-up focus. It's the coaching equivalent of the TV advertisement for a national newspaper where a young male is being chased down the street by a policeman. The viewer's assumption is that the youth is trying to escape arrest. It is only when the camera draws back that we see that the youth is rushing to save someone who is in danger of being crushed by falling scaffolding, and the policeman is following in his wake to offer support. The strap line 'a different perspective', is exactly what the Manager Coach is enabling when they spend time in establishing tangibles.

For some staff this will be enough. The recognition of the wider terrain will enable them to start moving towards identifying their goal and solutions for achieving it. For others it will be insufficient because they come not only with a narrow focus but also with assumptions that colour their view of themselves and the world. The A in the STARTED model signals the need to give time to exploring those assumptions that are blocking progress.

Assumptions sit in the subglacial territory; the holder does not refer to them because they behave as though they are self-evident truths. As a Manager Coach who is listening with intent, assumptions are constantly being revealed in the choices that people believe they have available to them.

A mantra of self-improvement states, 'whether you think you can or whether you think you can't, you're right'. In other words choose your assumption, and the actions will follow that prove your assumption correct. When John Kennedy announced to Congress in May 1961 that within a decade America would put a man on the moon, it is often quoted as evidence of visionary leadership. However, the starting point of that vision was the assumption that such a thing was possible. It was an assumption made in the face of overwhelming evidence that the Russian capability to achieve this was far greater than that of the USA.

As Kennedy said in a later speech, 'We choose to go to the moon, we choose to go to the moon in this decade and do the other things, not because they are easy, but because they are hard'.[1] He did not empirically know it could be done. The evidence of American space disasters in preceding years would have argued against the likelihood of success, but he used a positive assumption to drive actions that delivered that success. Often, people bring negative assumptions to coaching conversations that prevent the possibility of success.

Assumptions are leaked in assertions such as:

- 'It's not possible.'
- 'I can't.'
- 'No-one ever . . .'
- 'It's not realistic.'
- 'I don't have time.'

The assumption is then disguised by being wrapped in a velvet cloak that presents the resistance as reason:

- 'I would love to do that but it's not possible because it would upset . . .'
- 'I can't take on that work because I haven't been on the course.'
- 'I can see that it makes sense but no one ever does business with . . . and succeeds.'
- 'It's great in theory but it's not realistic to . . .'

The speaker edges up to the possibility of moving forward, and then the assumption leaps up to bite them and they are driven back.

Coaching FAST means getting those assumptions into the open so that their basis in truth can be explored, and alternative assumptions that will help solution-building can be identified.

Assumptions, assumptions, assumptions

Nancy Kline is a writer and coach who helps her clients to structure their thinking through confronting their assumptions. She states that 'the most tenacious block to a new idea is a limiting assumption'.[2] A coachee can have a very clear idea about what they want to achieve, but the fact that they are asking for some of your time to talk it through signals that they are holding assumptions that make it difficult for them to act. Those assumptions may be about themselves or about how the world operates. The task of the Manager Coach is to find out what they are.

In Kline's model of structured thinking, once the individual has signalled that they have a desired outcome but that they are not able to act on it, the listener hears the block and tests out the possibility of a limiting assumption through asking:

What might you be assuming that is stopping you from achieving what you want?

The choice of words is deliberate. It does not challenge the individual directly by saying. 'So what's getting in the way?', which can lead to more 'velvet cloak' speak. Instead, the inclusion of the word 'might' invites the speaker to be exploratory and to consider that there could be something there. The Manager Coach may suspect they know what that block is based on what they have already heard but, rather than stating it, they present the question in a spirit of curiosity.

The wording allows the individual to start considering possible barriers, and the listener encourages them to consider for as long as is helpful through using the quantum question '*What else?*'.

In just the same way that in brainstorming sessions the best ideas emerge towards the end of the session when people have settled into the task, removed their discomfort and let go of their top layer thinking, so the question 'What else?', allows the speaker to look again and again until they have exhausted their thinking and reached down beneath the surface. When that point is reached the listener can then ask the speaker to consider which of all the assumptions are most important to them.

It is here that the listener needs to pay close attention, because the choice will be key to the rest of the discussion. Whatever that key assumption is, Kline suggests it will fall into one of three categories:

- Fact
- Possible fact
- Bedrock assumption.

EXAMPLE

An ambitious young executive who says that they are keen for challenge talks about their desire to be moved around internationally. 'I would go anywhere', they claim, 'if it would give me a big enough challenge that would gain me some career credibility. I would even go to Baghdad'.

The coach asks them 'what are you assuming that stops you putting yourself forward for an assignment in Baghdad?'.

They could reply:

- *Fact* — there is no company office in Baghdad.
- *Possible fact* — this company would never open an office in Baghdad.
- *Bedrock assumption* — I'm not good enough to be considered for anything innovative such as setting up an office in Baghdad.

Facts are clear, the company either does or does not have an office in Baghdad. Possible facts are about events or people over which the individual does not have control. It is possible the company would never open an office in Baghdad, but it is not impossible. Most often, when assumptions are explored, the key assumption is not a fact or a possible fact, it is a bedrock assumption.

Bedrock assumptions are rocks in the brain, built up from layers of thinking that have been laid down over the years. They have a degree of impermeability that makes them facts of life rather than subjective thoughts. One of the reasons for using the 'What else?' question repeatedly, is that bedrock assumptions are unlikely to be the first thought that the speaker is willing to share. They are revealed once the top soil has been removed. Sharing bedrock assumptions requires courage on the speaker's part because such assumptions reveal so much. Bedrock assumptions relate to a self that is often never made available to others.

CASE STUDY

Martin was on a high-flyer programme, sitting alongside peers who were destined for Board membership. He worked for a global oil company, and had been told that he was likely to be appointed to a subsidiary Board within the year. He asked for a coaching session because he said he was unsure about continuing with the company. He talked about escaping to a different life in California, of giving up the corporate world and reclaiming parts of himself that had been sacrificed in building a successful career. He talked about his career having been a surprise to him because he had not gone to University and came from a very ordinary background. The coach sensed him as being caught between the chance of escape, and the chance to make it to the top of an organization he had committed his whole working life to. So they asked, 'What are you assuming that stops you from being able to fully commit to being a Board member?'. He offered a number of assumptions relating to the demands of the role, before answering a 'What else?' question with the response, 'I don't look and sound like those other people on the Board'.

His bedrock assumption was that a working-class boy, without the privileges of public school education and an Oxbridge degree, could never be accepted as a Board member.

To the outside world he looked like a supremely self-confident executive, but inside there was a layer of rock that prevented him viewing himself as acceptable to those whose backgrounds differed from his own. Once he owned the bedrock assumption he was able to start examining it for its truth, but whilst it lay in his head it was driving him to seek an escape route.

Bedrock assumptions come in two forms:

1. Those about the self:
   - I am not a leader
   - I am not clever enough
   - I don't have the confidence to
   - I have no influence
   - I don't deserve
   - I'm not political
   - I'm unlucky.

2. Those about the world and how it operates:
   - No clouds have silver linings
   - No pain no gain
   - You must always finish what you start
   - The only person you can rely on is yourself
   - At the end of every dark tunnel there is another train rushing to mow you down
   - It's who you know not what you know.

Discovering the bedrock assumption is gold-dust for the Manager Coach because it provides the material from which an alternative assumption can be built.

For all the time that the assumption is a sedimentary layer hidden from view, it is impossible to challenge it. Once an individual has the courage to share their bedrock assumption, the Manager Coach's responsibility is to offer them a tool they can use to break it up. It is here that Challenge for Thought is offered, through using a different thinking framework from the one that the assumption holder clings to.

There is no point challenging a bedrock assumption with objective data in the hope that this will overwhelm the person's subjectivity. A bedrock assumption that the person is not 'good enough' to be appointed to a job will not be smashed by saying, 'Of course you are good enough. I have seen your IQ results from your Development Centre'. A bedrock assumption that the person is not 'likable', will not be removed by stating, 'Just look at how many people sponsored you on that charity bike ride, you must be likeable'. Breaking up the bedrock assumption comes from offering an alternative positive philosophical mindset. This is different from the mindless optimism of, 'Of course you can do it'. A positive philosophical mindset assumes that people think better when offered a positive framework than when offered a negative one, so the coach encourages them to create one.

EXAMPLE

A staff member who has been contributing little at departmental meetings, and has admitted they feel uncomfortable, is asked what they might be assuming that is stopping them contributing. They reveal very quickly that their bedrock assumption is that their ideas are less important than other people's.

The Manager Coach holds back from saying, 'Of course your ideas are as important as everyone else's. I would just like to hear more of them' or even, 'Just get over it and stop holding back'. Instead they invite them to create a positive and *true* alternative to their existing assumption. This is not necessarily a polar opposite.

The polar opposite of 'my ideas are less important than other people's', would be 'my ideas are more important than other people's'. This may not sit comfortably. A positive and true alternative could be:

'My ideas are as important as . . .' or *'My ideas deserve hearing.'*

The words are those of the assumption holder, never the coach.

Once the positive alternative assumption has been identified then the coach, having listened closely, uses them to frame what Nancy Kline calls the 'incisive question':[3]

'If you knew that your ideas are as important as everyone else's what would you do at the next project meeting?'

The Manager offers the invitation to the staff member to allow themselves the possibility of being as important as everyone else, because, in so doing, they will be freed up to think of what it is possible for them to do. They do not have to accept that they are, but the question encourages the idea that in playing with that possibility, they can discover their resourceful self.

This is purposefully different from using their existing assumption framework. Applying that framework the Manager Coach would say, 'Knowing that your ideas are not as important as everyone else's what can you do at the next project meeting?' – to which the answer has to be 'Nothing'.

The language here is important. The Manager Coach is suggesting in the question: just try this idea out and see if anything emerges from thinking this way that is different from your usual process. It is not forced positive thinking: 'day by day in every way I am getting better and better'. It is a pragmatic recognition that the human brain works best when making a positive choice about oneself and one's situation. It's the difference between the impossibility of a situation that overwhelms us when we are tired, and the possibilities that become available to us after a good night's sleep, when the brain has had time to process and rebalance thinking.

Working with bedrock assumptions is a core Challenge for Thought skill. It requires the Manager Coach to restate the assumption through asking a question that shifts perspective.

A challenge can also be provided when the assumption is presented as a possible fact. Here the qualifier 'might' is often used to mask an assumption:

- 'They might think I am acting out of turn.'
- 'They might not want me.'
- 'I might not be good enough.'
- 'I might cry.'
- 'They might not care.'

Bedrock Assumption	Positive True Alternative	Challenge for Thought
I am not a leader	I can lead when I believe in the goal	If you knew that you can lead when you believe in the goal, what would you want to do about ...?
I'm not clever enough	I am clever enough for most things	If you knew you are clever enough for most things, what would you ...?
I've got no confidence	I have got enough confidence	If you knew you have enough confidence what would you be doing about ...?
I have no influence	I have got some influence	If you knew you have some influence how would you use it to ...?
I don't have the right ...	I have some rights within my role	If you knew you have some rights within your role, how would you use them to ...?
I'm totally unpolitical	I have good intuition about things	If you knew you have good intuition about things, how could you use that now to ...?
I'm unlucky	I have as much luck as the average Joe	If you knew you have as much luck as the average Joe, what would that enable you to do about ...?

Figure 7.1 Challenges for thought

An instinctive response to hearing a 'might' statement is to challenge with a 'might not', in the hope of shifting thinking over the line into a more positive framework. This appears to be positive, but it leaves the Manager Coach leading the other's thinking, rather than stimulating it. Applying the incisive questioning framework, the Manager Coach can ask:

- 'If you knew you are not acting out of turn what would you do?'
- 'If you knew they want you what would that enable you to do?'
- 'If you knew you are good enough what would that make possible?'
- 'If you knew you would not cry what would you say?'
- 'If you knew they did care how could that help you to ... ?'

Extending it further, it can even be applied to facts of assumption.

Fact
There is no office in Baghdad.

Coaching question
'If there was an office in Baghdad, what would it be like if it was giving you the sort of challenge you are seeking.'

Coach's positive intent
Since you are right that there is no office in Baghdad, help me understand what you are wanting from an assignment, so we can look for other possibilities.

Fact
There is a ban on increasing headcount.

Coaching question
'If the ban was not there how would you be using that additional headcount?'

Coach's positive intent
To encourage consideration of what they want to achieve with additional resource and how much of that can be achieved in the present circumstances.

Fact
No one under thirty has ever been appointed a Regional Director.

Coaching question
'If a Regional Director under thirty was appointed, what would you be doing now to prepare yourself for the role?'

Coach's positive intent
To shift the focus to how they can further their development and so increase their internal marketability, regardless of whether a specific role is available to them.

EXERCISE
Identify for yourself an issue where you are currently not taking action, although you have a sense of what you want to do. This could relate to work, e.g. a difficult conversation you are avoiding, or your personal life, e.g. not dealing with an underlying tension in a friendship.

Having identified the issue, ask yourself the question:

'What am I assuming that stops me from ...'

List your assumptions, prompting yourself with 'What else?' until you run out of ideas.

Then ask yourself to identify the assumption that is most important for you as a limitation on your actions.

Having identified the assumption classify it. Is it:

- A fact
- Possible fact
- Bedrock assumption.

Having identified the core assumption then construct what, for you, is an alternative and true assumption.

Use that positive assumption to construct your incisive question,

'If I knew that ... what would I do about ...'

List the possibilities that arise from taking a positive philosophical mindset. What becomes available to you that was not available when you were working from the negative assumption?

Using a matrix to unearth assumptions

The structured-thinking model encourages the thinker to expose the limitations of their assumption and to see the possibilities that come from challenge. An alternative approach is to go along with the assumption and to allow the individual to look at how the assumption plays out within a structured framework. This can be more comfortable for some coachees.

The matrix (Figure 7.2) allows for exploring the consequences and risks of taking and not taking action towards a desired outcome.

Offering the framework encourages the identification of assumptions both about the self and the wider context, which then allows for an assessment of how willing the individual is to be limited by the assumption.

What are the possible consequences of doing?	What are the possible consequences of not doing?
What are the possible personal risks in doing?	What are the possible personal risks in not doing?

Figure 7.2　Structured thinking matrix

CASE STUDY

Joe was a middle manager in a local authority who had recently been appointed to head up a team where one of the team members was underperforming. She had been in the department for over 20 years. She had a strong personality and often intimidated younger staff. By virtue of her time in the department, she had personal relationships with Senior Managers up the line. Joe came to his coaching discussion with a desire to begin performance-managing her, but with an underlying assumption that she had too much history for him to be able to discipline her.

When he talked the issue through using the matrix given in Figure 7.2 he identified the information given in Figure 7.3.

When Joe looked at the issue in this way, he started from assumptions that encouraged him to do nothing: possible alienation from the team; lack of capability in carrying it out; that doing nothing was better than doing something. The more he considered 'What else?', the closer he moved to assumptions that provided a case for addressing the issue: the possibility of recognition; his own sense of failure if he avoided action; the signalling to others that he could deal with the difficult aspects of people management. In the discussion using the framework the word

What are the possible consequences of doing?	What are the possible consequences of not doing?
• I am alienated from the rest of the team who will side with her out of fear • I am challenged by more Senior Managers to back off • I get recognition for taking something on that others have avoided • I get recognition for showing that I take performance management seriously	• None – people accept her as she is, so no one expects anything to change • I am viewed as a poor manager and it impacts on my performance review rating • I make things worse for the person who follows me • I feel a failure because I have lacked the courage to act
What are the possible personal risks in doing?	What are the possible personal risks in not doing?
• I do it badly, and she appeals against me to HR • I am seen as an autocratic manager • I show that I can be tough rather than the easy going guy they normally see	• I am seen as ineffective by my team • I waste head count and so don't deliver on objectives • My own sense of self-confidence is affected by avoiding the issue

Figure 7.3 Joe's filled-in matrix

'assumption' was never used, but the framing of the questions in the boxes encouraged Joe to explore his assumptions.

Reframing

A third position from which assumptions can be challenged is one drawn from Neuro Linguistic Programming (NLP).[4] Reframing is about helping an individual to see their situation differently through putting a different frame on it. The coach offers a new interpretation of the situation, not because the new interpretation is right or better than the one held by the coachee but because, in offering a new interpretation, a new set of feelings or ideas becomes available.

What the coach did at every stage of the conversation in Figure 7.4, was to listen and then offer an alternative frame of interpretation so that the speaker had two pictures to look at. By being helped to reframe she could see that what she had to offer was of value, rather than a burden that trapped her. By being able to see a mother as having a different role at different stages of a child's life, she was able to find a way of getting her needs met.

Reframing means using the resistance rather than fighting it. It's not the push of an opposing perspective, it is about acknowledging the coachee's view, and then offering an alternative viewpoint.

In each reframe, the coach is modelling an alternate assumption, from which different actions flow. 'It is not possible' is put up against an alternative assumption that progress is possible when things are broken down into achievable chunks. If work is the problem, it is held up against an alternative assumption

Conversation	Coachee assumption	Coach's reframe
Staff member : I am sick of my job. I am fed up helping other people only to see them move on and I stay behind	He/she should feel sorry for me	
Manager Coach's response : You must be very good at supporting other people, even though I can see that you are tired of doing it		You have a skill which is available to you, but which you have been overusing
Staff member : Yes, I know I am good at it, my appraisal ratings are always good, but I don't want to do it any more. It is too easy for me to be dumped on	You owe it to me to let me stop doing this job	
Manager Coach's response : You get recognition for your support skills in your appraisal. Support skills are valuable, but I can see that when it feels like being dumped on it's hard to see any value. How could you get more recognition for them?		Why not look to build on what you have, rather than rejecting it
Staff member : It would mean getting more training so I support on more challenging stuff. How do I get that when I am the departmental 'mother' holding it all together?	It is not possible for me to change anything	
Manager Coach's response: You see yourself as the caring mother, and part of being a mother is about helping children to stand on their own two feet by not always doing everything		Think of the wider responsibilities of being a mother and how you can use them to work for you

Figure 7.4   Reframing

Staff member : I never think of it that way, I only think of it in terms of me being the one that has to pick up the dirty washing Manager Coach's response : If you are wanting to stop picking up the washing, what can you say to your staff?	I might be able to do something different if I could look at my role differently	You can take control
Staff Member : It's time you all took on some of the things I have been doing for you, so that I can take some time out to develop my skills Manager Coach's response : That sounds like a mother who wants her children to grow up and give her some space, but isn't rejecting them	I can speak out and assert my needs without having to walk away from my job	You have choices as to how you interpret the role of mother, without having to reject it totally

Figure 7.4 Continued

that there are areas of work that are not problematic. Inability to learn is challenged by an alternative assumption that age brings the benefits of learning. The reframe is offered as a means of opening up new thinking, never as a means of discounting their analysis.

CASE STUDY

Caroline was a mother of three young children who was working part time with a small PR agency. She had held a senior-level job in a much larger PR business, and the demands of her present role were well within her reach. She came to her coaching session complaining that her skills were not being fully used and resenting some of the more junior-level assignments she was being given. In particular she spoke of one on-going assignment where she felt little empathy with the client. At the same time she had decided she wanted to gain an expensive further qualification in order to expand her range of options. At the beginning of the session she saw the client organization as the enemy. If only she did not have to give time to them she could be involved in more challenging work. Through questioning on the tangibles, the coach established that this client was her major source of revenue. Using a reframe, the coach offered

'So this client could be the means by which you could have your further training?'. Caroline accepted the reframe, and built a picture where she saw the client as an enabler rather than a disabler. With this new frame of reference she re-engaged with them, and was more highly motivated to deliver a good service. In the process she stopped seeing what was not good enough about the level of the work, and saw instead what the work could provide for her. She reframed the work rather than defining herself by it.

Reframing asks that the coachee looks at what they regard as the problem, and consider what can be gained by working with it, rather than battling against it. This seems illogical, since it is that very thing that they have brought as their issue. However, the thing that they now see as a problem often started out as being an ally to them. It is as the individual changes in their motivations that they begin to see a block where once they saw a springboard. Because solution

The assertion	The assumption	The push back	Reframe
It will never work	I can't do that	Of course it will work, you just need to think positively	It won't be easy for you, but what in all of this, can you work on?
I'm totally fed up with my job	The job is the problem	Get real, it's better here than most places	I can see how you are feeling. What are you least fed up with?
I'm an old dog, you can't teach me new tricks	I can't learn	It's not an option not to learn	Old dogs have learnt a lot. What have you learnt that is relevant to what is happening in the business now?
I hate writing technical reports	Someone else should do this for me	It's a requirement that you do write reports. I will get you on a course	What comes most easily in writing reports? What specifically do you have difficulty with? How can you work on that?

Figure 7.5 Example

focused thinking never throws away previous evidence of skills and resourcefulness, the coach has a role in helping them look at what is useful in the very thing they claim to reject.

> ### CASE STUDY
>
> Lawrie had worked for over a decade as a corporate lawyer and professed that he had hated it from day one. However, he earned so much money that he could not consider escaping, since every form of escape meant a loss of income. He was caught in a loop that went: 'I hate being a lawyer but at least I am rewarded for my misery. If I did something more meaningful I would be poor, and if that other thing proved a bad move, I would be miserable and poor. Better, then, that I stay miserable and wealthy'. Reframing for him meant asking the question, 'How could you use being a lawyer to help you make the change?'.
>
> At first the question seemed illogical. However, since he had made the decision to be a lawyer based on some knowledge of his own abilities, it did reflect some part of him. The coach asked him to view it not as an unhealthy part of himself to be exorcized, but a partner in making changes. From this reframe he was able to identify:
>
> - He could do a less demanding job in law, which would free up time.
> - He could use that time to explore options.
> - He could still have a good standard of living while he moved towards a better-fit future.
> - Work did not have to be looked at in all or nothing polarities.
>
> The solution that emerged included law as a part of his life, but a different area of law. It was used along with other interests that were important to him. From the reframe challenge, he was able to find the part of himself where law had a place, rather than seeing law as the reason for his unhappiness.

Challenging the givens

So far, we have looked at assumptions as barriers to be overcome through the Manager Coach enabling the individual to name and then remove them.

The coachee is then able to discover the possibilities that are released by an alternative true assumption, or a reframe.

There is another role that a Manager Coach can play as a challenger to thought, which is to confront those things that individuals believe should not apply to them; the things that we each would like to believe are not true but are, in fact, givens of being human and working in organizations.

David Richo[5] calls these the five things we cannot change, and he names them as:

1. Everything changes and ends.
2. Things do not always go to plan.
3. Life is not always fair.
4. Pain is part of life.
5. People are not always loving and loyal.

Viewed from a distance, individuals will recognize the truth in all these givens, but when experiencing their impact directly, we barter.

Everything changes and ends	but please not until I am ready for it
Things don't always go according to plan	but I want to be in control of the plan
Life is not always fair	but it should be to me
Pain is part of life	but I'd rather avoid it
People are not loving and loyal all the time	but they should be to me

People want to believe those givens do not apply to them, even though they can see clearly how they apply to others.

- A colleague should just accept that the job is becoming redundant and move on to something new.
- A team member should understand that there are no promises about careers, all are dependent on business conditions, which regularly change.
- A friend should see that promotions are always about more than being the best performer.

- A direct report should recognize that any transition involves the pain of letting go and the uncertainty of what is coming next.
- A member of the sales team should not be surprised when customers go elsewhere even though you have worked your 'butt' off to meet their needs. That's life.

When it impacts on ourselves the perspective shifts, because the given is attacking our ego, and the ego fights back. In coming to a manager and discussing an issue they are struggling with, it is likely that at some point that person's ego will appear to complain against one of life's givens.

- 'It's not fair that …'
- 'It's too early for change.'
- 'This should not be happening. It wasn't in the plan.'
- 'This is really difficult for me.'
- 'I can't believe they could behave in that way when we are friends/ colleagues/mothers/doing the same job.'

In expressing the failure of the 'given' to be acted out, their hope is that the Manager Coach will provide reassurance that the given does not apply to them.

The challenge for the Manager Coach is to help the coachee to accept the given and then work with it, because to collude with the belief that it does not operate is to guarantee disappointment and frustration. This perspective does not sit easily with a prevailing assumption of the successful, that with enough will and effort outcomes can be controlled. However, life in organizations constantly shows that control is not a given. Things we value do end, and not always in ways that are comfortable. Complete control of an outcome is never possible. Unfair things do happen to people regardless of the number of policies put in place to prevent it. The demands of organizational life are painful at times, and good people sometimes do things that are uncaring. An alternative perspective drawn from Buddhism argues that it is in accepting the given that people can find new possibilities. It is when they deny the given that they become trapped by anger and frustration.

Having the courage to work with the given is particularly important when a coach is working within an organization. The Manager Coach holds a unique position in sitting between the organization and the individual.

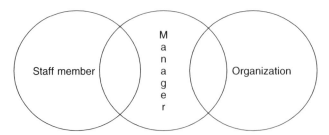

Figure 7.6 The Manager coach sits between the staff member and the organization

Occupying that position means that the Manager Coach has a responsibility to work with the organizational givens in fulfilling their coaching role.

Coaching to accept life's givens does not mean becoming a Buddhist. It means being able to challenge thought through holding a position that does not try to rescue the other person by giving false reassurances, or to protect themselves from the other's anger by supporting ideas that they know to be non-viable.

If we avoid acknowledging the givens, the Manager Coach is taking on the position of a parent who tries to protect their child from more than they think they can deal with. As a Manager Coach your role is not to provide protection from hurt or to judge how much truth a staff member can deal with, but to use the truth in ways that will help the coachee to ground themselves, and to be more capable of dealing with that truth.

Many years ago I worked within a University Careers Service. I stayed far too long in the job because it was a great town to live in and I was enjoying being single and having fun. In order to justify my lack of career progress I built the job up year by year, taking on more and more responsibilities. These took me further and further away from the core purpose of the role. I built a job that worked very well for me, and then I began to feel that my contribution was not being adequately financially rewarded. I began to see the University as being unfair to me, and I decided to confront the Dean on the matter. Armed with all the data on my contribution I sat down convinced he would back down before the evidence. He heard me out and then said, 'I can see that you are doing a lot of good things, and it seems unfair to you that you are not being paid extra for them. However, we don't need you to do many of those things you have decided you want to do. If you want recognition for them, you need to look elsewhere'.

I left the session enraged at his unwillingness to cede ground. With distance, I can see that what he did was to hold the ground between myself and the organization through signalling to me that my sense of unfairness was based on a model of what the organization should want of me, rather than what it did want of me.

In retrospect, it was a great piece of coaching. By challenging my thought he forced me to confront the lack of attention I had been giving to my own career, and within months I had left the University for a more appropriate role.

The myth of control

Underpinning much of the anger that individuals bring to coaching conversations is their belief in their power to control outcomes, and to live according to a defined plan. Holding onto the power of those beliefs guarantees a sense of failure.

I met a politician who had lost their parliamentary seat in an election, and was struggling to find a life beyond. At a rational level they knew that ultimately all political careers end in failure. At a personal level they could not accept it had happened to them. They remained angry at the unfairness of the system; the disloyalty of their constituents; at the timing of the ousting; and at the pain of no longer being sought out by others. They were trapped by their anger and a collapsed sense of self-worth, which they tried to avoid acknowledging by casting blame on others.

They had been ousted, but they would not accept it. They still wanted to believe that there was some way in which they could have controlled the result. Until they accepted that their political life was over, they were incapable of letting go and finding a satisfactory way of applying their considerable abilities.

The flip side of being trapped by being unable to exert control, is being able to see new possibilities through not having control.

Former athlete Roger Black, won two silver medals in the 1996 Olympics. Talking about the experience,[6] he highlighted that his success was made possible by the failure of life being delivered according to plan. Having not achieved the 'A' level grades he needed to go to medical school, he was left at home whilst most of his friends went off to University. With little to do, he accepted a friend's invitation to go along to the local running club, although he had never been involved in athletics. He went, quickly discovered he had some ability, and within a year was the European Junior Champion. He subsequently went to University to read medicine, but that disruption to the plan opened up possibilities that would never have been available to him if the original plan had been implemented.

Of course, it is easier for individuals to be open to changing plans when they have invested relatively little of themselves in the outcome, but when individuals overinvest in a plan they risk not noticing what else is available.

CASE STUDY

Stephen came to a coaching discussion with a clear purpose. He wanted to know what he needed to do to guarantee he would be Chief Executive of the construction firm he worked for within five years. On the surface it seemed a reasonable request. Given he had risen to the Board with stratospheric speed, and had been given a national award in recognition of his potential, it would have been easy to see the discussion as a simple diagnostic of the gap between his present skills and experience and the requirements of the CEO role. The coach resisted this because to follow his lead would have been to collude with the idea that life is totally in our control. Instead they asked, 'How do you know that the company will exist in five years time?'. Stephen bristled at this challenge to his assumption. He began a detailed explanation of the company's strategy and performance strength. The coach interrupted and said, 'I accept everything you say but, if you only offer yourself the possibility of being CEO for this company, your plan will be in tatters if unforeseen circumstances mean the role is not available to you. Given that the outcome is not totally under your control, what is it that being CEO of this company means for you?'. The challenge to his belief in the given of controlling outcomes through planning, allowed Stephen to begin to look at himself separate from the company. He was able to identify abilities and motivations separate from his corporate identity, and a more valuable development agenda emerged. He could find that, five years on, he is the CEO, but by confronting the given, he now had more possibilities open to him.

The Given	The Fear	The Behaviour	The Manager Coach's role	The Need	The Pay Off
Things change and end	I will lose what I have and what has defined me	Resistance to the change	To empathize, but not to deny the truth	To be allowed to express the emotions involved in letting go	The learning that they can deal with things ending, and the discovery that new things appear when we let go rather than trying to hold on
Things don't always go according to plan	I will feel out of control if the plan doesn't work out	Planning every detail as though the plan makes it immutable	To challenge through acknowledging that plans can fail to deliver, rather than trying to work on producing failsafe plans	To see what can be learnt from the failure of a plan	A freeing up so that they can see and respond to new possibilities
Things are not fair	I will be denied my fair share	Constant scanning for evidence of unfairness	To acknowledge their perception of unfairness without being caught into being the magician who can wave it away	To equip them to work around that reality, rather than raging against it	To equip them for a recognition that in organizational life, 'You win some and you lose some', the skill is in recognizing which ones really matter
Pain is part of life	I won't be able to deal with it	Avoidance of situations which they see as potentially difficult	To present confronting difficulty as the means by which they will be better equipped to deal with it	To be able to deal with difficult situations and remain centred, even while it is painful	To be effective in more challenging situations with potentially bigger rewards
People are not loving and loyal all the time	I will be hurt if they don't behave well towards me	Overconcern with pleasing others in the belief that this will avoid hurt	To confront the magic hope that pleasing others means they have to be nice back. To help them define what are helpful beliefs in working with others	To be able to acknowledge their own feelings and thoughts, which are not always loving and loyal	Being more real in how they deal with people, and in what they expect back from them

Figure 7.7 Challenging thoughts

The role of the Manager Coach is to offer the challenge found in Zen teaching, 'This being the case, how shall you proceed?'. The challenge is offered to enable the other person to hold the given up to the light, and explore the possibilities that follow.

In working with another's givens, you help the other person best by enabling them to accept reality, through using skills in challenging thought.

EXERCISE

Which of life's givens is impacting on how you are approaching a situation in your life right now?

How does the belief that the given should not apply to you, affect your feelings and behaviour?

If you accepted its truth, rather than trying to barter with it:

- What would change?
- What would it be possible for you to do, that you cannot do when resisting the given?

Summary

Collecting data on the situation as it impacts on an individual is enriched if you can help the coachee to acknowledge the assumptions they bring to their situation. By bringing those assumptions to the surface the Manager Coach can help the coachee to:

- Create a true, positive alternative that frees up thinking and the identification of solutions.
- Examine the assumptions implicit in their assessment of possible consequences and personal risk.
- Reframe their thinking so that they assess a situation differently.
- Acknowledge when their assumption is based on refusing to accept one of life's givens.

References

1. John F. Kennedy, speech made at Rice University, 12 September 1961. Speech available at http://www.nasa.gov.

2. Kline, N. (1999) *Time to Think*. Ward Lock, p. 166.
3. Kline, N. *op cit.*, p. 177.
4. McDermott, I. and Jago, J. (2001) *The NLP Coach*. Piatkus.
5. Richo, D. (2005) *The Five Things We Cannot Change*. Shambhala Publishing.
6. Roger Black, keynote address at the Academy of Executive Coaching Conference, January 2004.

8

Reality bites

What you see and hear depends a good deal on where you are standing.

C.S. Lewis

The previous chapter looked at how to unearth and challenge assumptions. By doing so, the ground may now be prepared to start working towards solutions, or there may still be a niggling doubt in your mind. You have helped your staff member describe their tangibles by your use of quantum questions. In listening to their replies you recognize that there is more to this than they have told you. While perception is their reality, there are other realities that it would be useful to bring to their attention. It is here that the R, of Reality Bites, comes into play.

Back in the 1950s two men, Joseph Luft and Harry Ingham, working at the Western Training Laboratory in the USA, developed a way of looking at how people reveal themselves. The framework they designed was named the Johari Window,[1] and it has been a mainstay of interpersonal skills training programmes for the last forty years (Figure 8.1). It has survived because it highlights how partial our realities are, and that becoming more skilful in our relationships comes from gaining more information about ourselves. This happens through bringing into the open things that previously have been hidden from view both to ourselves and others.

Coaching is a fast-track way of opening up the Johari window, because it encourages individuals to reveal more about themselves and provides a structure to reduce unknown areas.

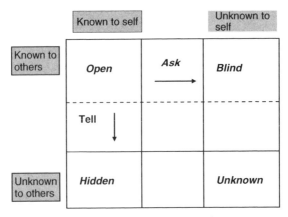

Figure 8.1 The Johari window

The Open zone is the part of our conscious self, our attitudes, behaviour, motivations, skills and values of which we are aware. This is 'our open book' area. We recognize it ourselves and others recognize it in us. When a coaching conversation begins, the coachee is likely to start from offering information that is in the open area. As the coach listens with intent and builds rapport, a growing trust will encourage increased self-disclosure and they will begin to talk about feelings and thoughts that are usually hidden from others, although they are very familiar to them. The skill the coach shows at the Set Up stage will influence the degree to which the coachee begins to disclose from the Hidden zone. At some point, the listener will become aware that the coachee also has Blind areas. They will recognize it in the selectivity of how they talk about a problem and their part in it. Without that blind area being lifted the coachee's ability to come to a successful solution will be limited. It is here that the Manager Coach's role is to help increase their view of reality, and it is this that is the focus of this chapter. The final zone, that where the other person discovers that they are more than they know themselves, or that others know, can be one of the serendipitous rewards of coaching. Suddenly they gain an insight that they had not previously had and, in hearing that insight, the Manager Coach learns something they had not known before. That is one of the rewards of coaching someone you manage.

In looking at assumptions we were seeking to find what was hidden, and how it could be changed by bringing it into the light. In looking at reality bites, you are working to correct the stigmatism that is limiting their ability to see the full picture.

Changing the position on reality

When an individual tells their story, they are telling it from the position they have taken up. We hear it in whether they talk of themselves as a victim or a fighter for fairness, as a challenger of the status quo or a thwarted genius. They have also taken up a position within the story, since their story will involve a cast of at least one other who also has their own reality. That is a position they talk of less readily, because their investment is in their own role. Just as when an actor is given a part their first act is to go rapidly through the script seeing how many lines they have, so when a member of staff brings their issue, what they bring is their part within that situation. By the time they bring it into the open they will have developed a fully formed character. They have learnt their own lines, but they have not considered the meaning of those lines in terms of the whole play. For this reason, a number of helping therapies, including Gestalt and NLP, have highlighted the importance of helping an individual to look at their situation from a number of positions.

John Grinder and Judith De Lozier[2] describe three positions that are available to use when helping an individual to look at their situation.

First position

This is ourselves describing what we think, feel, see and hear. We present this as truth, and the coach using quantum questions helps expand that truth through establishing how often the problem occurs: where, with whom, the size of the difficulty and its impact.

Second position

This position asks the coachee to put themselves in the shoes of the person who is causing them difficulty. To experience not just what the other person is thinking, but to imagine how the situation looks from their seat; how they hear their words and how they feel. By asking a coachee to move out of first position and to take up the other's position, they are able to see the other person's map of the world, rather than only having access to their own. Powerful insights come from being forced to sit in a position that ordinarily they never access.

CASE STUDY

Francesca was a thirty-something, high-energy, talented middle manager. She hated being asked questions or challenged on her work because she saw it as her turf. She was in a specialist role, with knowledge her boss did not hold. To her that justified her protectionist attitude. She came to a coaching session furious that her boss had told her to take a different direction on a project she had been working on. He had explained that the issue cut across several areas of his responsibility and her approach was too narrow. From her perspective the reality was clear:

- I know more than he does.

- He is intrusive and unhelpful.
- There is no case for stepping into my territory.

The purpose she brought to the session was how she could influence him to back off and leave her alone. The coach did not challenge the purpose of the session at this stage, but asked her to put herself in his shoes and experience what it was like to manage Francesca. From this position she recognized:

- Francesca puts up barriers.
- It's difficult to get her to listen to any input once she sees the issue as her specialism.
- I have a responsibility for the outcome of Francesca's work, so I can't just let her have it her way.

Sitting in his place she also experienced that:

- He had twenty years experience as a Senior Manager.
- He had much wider responsibilities than Francesca's brief, and looked at issues from multiple perspectives.
- He had the right to ask questions.

When Francesca had experienced the second position, her coach took her back to her first position and asked her, 'What do you now see that you did not see before?'. She poured out a series of insights:

- That he had the right to manage.
- That he had a wider knowledge base than her own.
- That he only challenged when the issue cuts across areas. When it was a single area issue he trusted her judgement.

The coach was then able to return to the issue of purpose and ask her again, 'What is your purpose now?'. She replied, 'To find a way of working with him that uses what he has to offer me'.

With these new insights she was able to go back to her boss and ask for his help in getting her thinking in line with what was needed. She was able to appreciate his experience in leadership and to look for ways of learning from it, rather than rebelling against it.

Third position

Sometimes moving between two positions is enough to provide the reality bite from which new actions can emerge. At times it is helpful to add a third position. This is particularly true when someone is involved in a difficult relationship where both sides are caught in a dynamic that they cannot get out of.

Asking someone to take on a third position demands that they step away from both sides and look at them as a detached observer. From that distance they have a view that is not available close up.

CASE STUDY

Roger had a fraught relationship with his boss. Roger saw himself as a creative free spirit, and his boss as an anal, pedantic, detail freak. His response to his boss's desire to know what was happening, when and how, was to deflect answering through throw-away lines. He would deliberately describe a situation in a way that he knew would increase his boss's anxiety, just for the pleasure of frustrating him. His boss's response, inevitably, was to become ever more anxious and demanding of information. They were caught in a vicious cycle where each behaved in ways that brought out the worst in the other.

From the second position, Roger could see that his boss experienced him as undermining and that, feeling discounted, he saw shouting louder as the only way of being heard. However, even with this perspective, he would quickly flip back into his own position, counter-arguing from his positional evidence of how his boss's behaviour damaged his own self-worth.

The way out of this tug of war was to ask Roger to take up a third position, to stand outside the two of them and describe what he saw. When he stood in a third position Roger found a different perspective. From here he saw:

- Two colleagues who had similarities beneath the surface. They both shared a passion for their work.
- Two men who liked each other when they were not embattled.
- Two men who were making themselves stressed by what was happening between them.

Taking in a third position as a basis for expanding perceived reality, allowed Roger to identify new options available to him in his response to his boss. He was able to start identifying what were reasonable demands of him, rather than dismissing them all as unreasonable. He was able to look at his boss as a human rather than a demon, and to recognize the cost of the existing dynamic for the two of them.

Fourth position

Often two or three positions are enough, but there can be added value in adding in a fourth position as an additional reality bite.[3] The fourth position is one where the coachee is asked to consider how their thoughts and behaviours look from the perspective of a larger system. This can be particularly useful when the staff member has unrealistic expectations of the organization.

EXAMPLE

A direct report views their career as something that they alone manage. They claim that they have no expectations of the organization, because everyone has to manage their own future. Implicit in their view of reality is that they decide what they want and it is the organization's responsibility to provide it. They ask for a conversation about their career, and lay out what they are now wanting and by when. They see self-management as meaning control of the outcome.

Rather than offering them information on career prospects, which they may well resist, an alternative is to ask them to take up the position of being the organization. When they look at the issue of their career from the position of the organizational system what do they see and hear that adds to their understanding?

A fourth position does not have to be the organization, but it is a position for looking at things that impact from a wider system than the self. It could be relevant to help them look at the potential implications of a restructuring from the perspective of internal customers, or of a planned strategy from the client system on which it will impact.

As a Manager Coach you are listening for the position taken up by the other person, in order to identify the limitations placed on reality-checking by this position. You then can provide a reality bite by introducing one or more new positions from which to view their situation.

EXERCISE

Think of a minor irritation in your life – perhaps one of those on-going arguments that happen in relationships and friendships. An area where you have assumed a position of moral superiority, e.g. the other person's lack of punctuality, untidiness, inability to use the telephone.

Now put yourself in the other's shoes and imagine how the situation looks and feels from their position.

What is different when you take up their position?

Take a third position and look at the two of you from a distance. From this position, what do you see that is not visible close up?

Finally, if appropriate, consider the issue from a fourth position. What difference does it make to how you look at the situation when you consider the wider system impact? What is the impact of your behaviour when looked at from the perspective of a work team, your family, your sports team?

Searching for exceptions

When an individual seeks out help it is likely that they have been living with the issue for some while. During that time the script will have been rewritten many times in their head and, just as in Hollywood movies, in each rewriting the main themes will have become sharpened and less complex. Characters will be good or bad. In talking of their part the coach will hear absolutes. I 'always …' or I 'never …', 'I can't …' and 'It's impossible for me'.

On hearing those words, the Manager Coach has a clue that the need is to find exceptions to those absolutes, because it is in finding those exceptions that solutions emerge.

Insoo Kim Berg, a pioneer of Brief Therapy, describes exceptions as, 'those past experiences in a client's life when the problem may reasonably be expected to have occurred, but somehow did not'.[4] Implicit in this thinking is that no problem is there all of the time. Everyone has times when the problem is either not present or at least not there to the same degree.

Think of the number of times we hear the words 'Always' and 'Never'.

- 'I always forget detail.'
- 'I never remember names.'
- 'I always mess up in front of . . .'
- 'I never get recognition for my input.'
- 'I always miss out on the best projects.'
- 'I never understand what is going on in meetings.'

The speaker has developed a story line in which those assertions are solid realities. Change comes from challenging their solidity.

The simple repetition of the words 'never' and 'always' in a tone of voice that suggests incredulity, can be the starting point for finding those exceptions.

> *Coach:* You *always* forget detail?
>
> *Coachee:* OK not always, but I forget detail that isn't important to me.

The coach now has evidence that the individual is capable of retaining detail. The issue is one of motivation, not incapacity.

> *Coach:* You *never* get recognition for your input?
>
> *Coachee:* Well almost never. A couple of years ago I felt that people were seeing what I had to offer, and I felt much better about my work.

The coach now knows that this individual has had some positive feedback on their work. The need is to help them see what they were doing at that time, that made people more willing to give them acknowledgement.

In taking it a step further, the coach now looks to help them find recent examples of the 'exception' on show, so that they can learn from it. It is more useful to seek out recent examples, because the retention of detail will be both richer and more accurate. The coach leads them into the exploration by asking the other person 'Can you think of a time recently when you . . . remembered detail even though it was not important to you/got recognition for a piece of your work/did not mess up in front of . . ./understood what was going on in a meeting?'.

The explicit request to identify the exception allows for enabling them to describe what they did that was different from their usual actions, and 'how' they managed to do the exception. Once a person recognizes both that the exception exists, and can acknowledge how they did it, they have access to information that will help them do it again.

EXAMPLE

A staff member has admitted that the reason they are failing to meet the deadlines they have been set is that, when the pressure is on, they become so anxious that they paralyse their ability to act. They become overwhelmed by the deadline rather than being motivated by it. The Manager Coach, hearing the implicit 'always' in their story, asks them an exception question, 'Can you think of a time recently when you have been under pressure and not paralysed yourself?'. Reluctantly, they admit that in the last two weeks when they have been putting together next year's budget, although they have mostly felt anxiously unproductive, there was one day when the pressure did not knock them off balance, and they went home feeling they had achieved something (*evidence of the exception*).

The Manager Coach reflects back that it is possible for them to have a productive day even during a time of pressure, and asks them, 'what did you do that day?' (*quantum question that assumes they have some control over their anxiety*).

They answer:

- 'I got up that day feeling more relaxed because I had had a good night's *sleep*, because I got some *exercise* the previous day.'
- 'I said to myself, I am going to just *focus* on *one thing* today, rather than trying to make progress on everything.'
- 'I decided that if I just *did*, and *stopped worrying about* whether everything I did was *good enough*, I would get through more.'
- 'I made some time to have *lunch* with some friends who work in another department, rather than grabbing a sandwich at my desk, because I usually feel guilty if I am not working every minute of the day.'

The Manager Coach has now learnt that the exception occurred because there was deliberate thought and action on the part of his staff member. By the coach reflecting back the deliberate actions they brought to creating a productive, less anxious day, the staff member will more easily be able to access them again.

Of course the staff member could answer: 'I have no idea why it was a better day, maybe my bio-rhythms were working for me'. In this instance, they are suggesting it was random, and therefore unlikely to be repeated. A check of the degree of randomness can be made by the Manager Coach, offering another reality bite:

'If I asked a colleague of yours who saw you on that less anxious day, what they saw and heard you doing differently, what would they say?'

This allows the staff member a second opportunity to reflect. It is inviting them to move into the third position of observing themselves, through using the intermediary of a colleague. From here they might say:

- 'They would have noticed that I *wasn't constantly moving* from one pile of *paper* to another.'
- 'They would have noticed that I was away from my desk for 45 minutes when I went for *lunch* – which is unusual for me.'
- 'They would have heard me *having a laugh* on the phone with a friend, rather than ignoring phone calls because I think they are just bringing me more aggro.'
- 'They would have noticed that I *sat at my desk* for a lot of the day, rather than constantly moving around.'
- 'They would have noticed I was *quieter*; I wasn't swearing as much that day.'
- 'They would have seen that *I went home earlier than usual,* and I looked happier at the end of the day. I did not have that "I must have a drink to reward me for surviving the day look".'

By taking up the third position, the staff member is again able to identify a range of behaviours they used that day that are replicable.

If the staff member is adamant that the exception really was random, then probe further to find another example of a time when the problem did not occur. It will be there.

Central to looking for exceptions is the unearthing of as much data as possible on the 'how' of their behaving exceptionally. Because individuals are not used to talking in such detail about their actions, this can feel uncomfortable. They fear that their actions look so trivial that they can be of no interest or relevance, so it is important that the coach shows that they are both interested and want more. Insoo Kim Berg is known for using a voice of positive incredulity when her clients start talking of their exceptions, 'Wow', being a favourite response. This may not sit well with your style, but you need to find positive expressions that help the speaker tell you as much detail as they can recall, because in doing so they are mining resources that they can use again.

SAMPLE DIALOGUE

Coachee: I got up that day feeling more relaxed. I had had a good night's sleep because I got some exercise the previous day.

Coach: It's good that you managed to find some time for exercise which helped you sleep. How did you do that?

Coachee: I did not allow myself to go the pub with my friends as a reward for a hard day, because I knew if I did that exercise would go out the window.

Coach: What else did you do that day that made it different?

Coachee: I said to myself, I am going to just focus on one thing today, rather than trying to make progress on everything.

Coach: That sounds as though it helped. How did you that?

Coachee: I cleared my desk of everything that did not relate to my one thing, otherwise I knew I would distract myself.

Coach: That obviously worked. What else?

Coachee: I switched off the noise on the emails so I did not know when a new one had arrived.

Coach: That's so simple and yet it made a difference?

Coachee: It did, because it was me saying to myself, I don't want to be distracted.

Coach: You were clearly taking control that day. What else did you do?

> *Coachee:* I decided to just get something down on paper, rather than worrying if it was good enough.
>
> *Coach:* That sounds like a good strategy. What other things helped?
>
> *Coachee:* I made a list of what I had achieved so far in terms of delivering the budget, so that I had a sense of achievement I could build on, rather than only seeing what I had not done.
>
> *Coach:* That is such a good idea. It sounds as though it helped your motivation to do more.
>
> *Coachee:* It did, and then I felt that it was OK to have lunch with friends because I could see that I was making progress.
>
> *Coach:* You really made that day different. What else do you recall?
>
> *Coachee:* I think that's it.

By affirming the actions that the staff member took, and signalling interest with the 'what else?' question, the coachee has been able to identify a range of repeatable behaviours that otherwise would have been discounted. Centrally, they have recognized that their view of every day as being equally pressured and unproductive is only a partial view of reality.

When talking through exceptions, individuals tend to minimize their importance and want to return to the problem. 'Well one good day set against ninety awful ones isn't much.' In holding onto the good day, the coach is not dismissing the problem, but knows that they will not build momentum towards change by focusing on it. Change comes from drawing attention to what they have already done to create a shift in the right direction; by magnifying those things the coachee makes them more available for future use.

The skills of exception finding are:

- Ask the exception-seeking question: 'Can you think of a time recently when ...?'
- Asking for details on the 'what?' of the behaviour difference, and the 'how?' of their achieving it.
- Magnifying exceptions even when the coachee seeks to minimize them.
- Reflecting back the skills they have used and affirming them.

SAMPLE DIALOGUE

Val had spent her first year in a managerial role in an international leisure organization after several years in a management consultancy. She was struggling with changing from being the deliverer of ideas to the deliverer of outcomes. Her first performance review had not gone well and she knew her credibility was fast disappearing in an organization that was highly pragmatic and task-focused. When she talked about it with her coach she saw the problem as her inability to take the lead role. She saw herself as very good at taking the lead from a powerful individual and responding to it, but not comfortable taking the space herself. She was asking herself whether she was meant to manage, or should go back into consultancy. Her coach ignored the offer to discuss the pros and cons of leaving management, and asked her instead:

Coach: Have there been any times in the last few weeks when you have felt you have been a manager?

Val: Well, only once in a tiny way. (*Minimization of exception*)

Coach: Tell me about it.

Val: I had found that the meetings I was holding were great at generating ideas, which I love, but nothing was ever being followed up. I left thinking I had made it clear that actions should be taken, but no-one else seemed to have heard that. I could feel my frustration building up.

Coach: Talking about ideas began to feel inappropriate. So what did you do?

Val: At the next meeting I decided things had to be different, and they were. (*Exception identified*)

Coach: It's good you took the responsibility for making it different. What did you do?

Val: I did not really think about it at the time. (*Random?*)

Coach: And in retrospect what do you see?

Val: I can see that I did a few things differently.

Coach: What were they?

Val: I sent an email out before the meeting saying that my expectation was that by the end of the meeting we would have some clear agreements on actions, and that I wanted to use the meeting for that, rather than for any further discussion of ideas.

Coach: That's pretty clear. You made people understand what you expected of them. And what else?

Val: Then when we got together I did an up-front piece where I said we had some great discussions, which I had enjoyed, but it was time to focus on committing to action, and how we were going to deliver.

Coach: So you did not discount the previous meetings but you signalled a new purpose.

Val: Then I got everyone to contribute, and as a group we identified the critical deliverables, the tasks involved and timelines.

Coach: It's good that you were able to involve everyone in moving things forward against your purpose. What else did you do?

Val: I asked the people I judged most appropriate to take responsibility for those tasks.

Coach: So you clearly identified who was responsible for actions.

Val: And I gave some deadlines for next steps, and said if people disagreed we needed to discuss it now, as I expected people to be accountable to those deadlines.

Coach: You made your expectations clear and then allowed them to negotiate within those expectations.

Val: It felt much better than other meetings I have had, but I have only done it once. I could tell you about some terrible meetings I have had since.

Coach: I hear that it was only once, but let me summarize what you did, as it sounds as though you did step up to managing your team. I heard you say that you made your outcome expectations clear, and having done that you involved everyone in contributing to that purpose. You assigned tasks and you asked people to be accountable once they had accepted the timeframe. What in that could be helpful to you right now?

The coach brought Val to the point where she recognized that she is capable of taking the lead as a manager because she has done so. Those behaviours need repetition for her to become more comfortable with them, but Val's view of reality that she cannot manage has been challenged.

EXERCISE

Think of a situation that for you is a Never or Always situation, e.g.

- I never enjoy Christmas.
- I always have terrible holidays.
- I never get my point of view across.
- I always avoid conflict.

Ask yourself to think of a recent time when that was not true (or marginally less true).

Use the exception to explore:

- When was that?
- What did you do?
- How did you do that?

In getting data on the exception, what emerges that is useful for dealing with the same situation in the future?

Expanding reality through feedback

So far in looking at reality, the focus has been on expanding the open area within the Johari window, through bringing into the open information that the coachee had hidden away. Through asking them to assume alternative positions, they have come to realize that their understanding of reality is expanded when they think from more than their own perspective. By encouraging them to seek exceptions, they have been able to add colour to their black and white view of reality, and so find previously hidden resources.

These two skills are powerful in increasing the zone of reality awareness, but there are times when the coachee needs more. They need the reality bite that comes from addressing their blind area. The area where others know something of which the coachee is unaware. As a coach you recognize that if they just operate from their own reality, they will set themselves inappropriate goals. It is here that the coach has a responsibility to offer feedback.

For the Manager Coach this is a difficult issue. Inevitably, as their Manager you have a view of them that may not match with their view of themselves. However, to impose that view could break the trust they have in you or derail the conversation. It is here that the Manager Coach has to hold the purpose of coaching in mind. 'Two people working together for the benefit of one', means that the feedback given by the Manager Coach has to be offered with certainty that it will be of benefit to the issue that the coachee is wanting to address. There will be many forms of feedback that you could offer, but the feedback that is valuable in a coaching conversation is that which is specific to the coachee's intention.

Contrast these two conversations:

The staff member has asked for help in managing upwards, as they feel they are not good at behaving in appropriate ways with more Senior Managers. You offer to help them.

Version 1:

> *Coachee:* I know I upset the MD last week. Did he say anything to you?
>
> *Coach:* He said you are insensitive, and he did not want you fronting any meetings with major clients because you don't know how to gauge the mood and are heavy-handed.
>
> *Coachee:* He thinks I am useless. What do you think?
>
> *Coach:* I think you need to change your behaviour or you are in trouble.
>
> *Coachee:* What can I do?

Version 2:

> *Coachee:* I know I upset the MD last week. Did he say anything to you?
>
> *Coach:* How do you know you upset the MD?

Coachee: He ignored me at the end of the meeting, and I saw him bridle a number of times when I spoke.

Coach: Can you remember when he bridled?

Coachee: He looked uncomfortable when I pointed out the flaws in what the client was asking of us. I know that is not his style.

Coach: So your sense is that he did not like you challenging their thinking so openly?

Coachee: I am sure he thinks I am like a bull in a china shop. Do you think the same?

Coach: Are you asking me for feedback?

Coachee: I think it would help.

Coach: Would you like some feedback on how I see you behaving in meetings with external clients, or how I see you behaving with the MD?

Coachee: I guess it's how it is with him, because if I can't get it right, my career is going nowhere.

Coach: What I saw in that meeting was that you cut across him a number of times, and that when he signalled that he wanted to move things forward you ignored him, and carried on challenging their thinking.

Coachee: I did not even know I was doing that, I was so engrossed in my own thoughts.

Coach: So when you cut off from others and only listen to your own voice, you risk upsetting the MD. Can you think of a time when you have had a meeting with him when you have not behaved in that way?

The first invitation for feedback was heard by the Manager Coach as an opportunity to say things that had previously been kept from the staff member. It is the corridor conversation feedback, where people are labelled, and that label is attached to all their behaviours. The coachee now knows that he is seen as insensitive and in career trouble, but is no closer to knowing what he can do differently.

In the second, the Coach holds back from offering feedback until they are clear on what the context of the feedback is. Once they are clear that the feedback that would be helpful is related to improving the coachee's relationship with the MD, they offer specific feedback based on observation. The coachee is now clear on what he does that causes irritation, rather than how he is labelled. Understanding what he does when the relationship does not work allows for looking for evidence of behaviours he uses in other situations that could be used when working with the MD.

Feedback is particularly tricky for the Manager Coach, because it is tempting to use the opening as an opportunity to offload from their own agenda, and to say those things they have held back from saying. The Manager Coach has to constantly ask themselves the questions:

- How does this feedback serve the purpose of the conversation?
- Am I offering feedback that should be addressed within a performance review discussion?

If the answer is that the feedback primarily serves the Manager Coach's purpose, or that it is feedback that they have avoided giving in performance discussions, then it has no place in a coaching conversation.

CASE STUDY

Henry was a graduate trainee in an investment bank, who was eager to get on quickly. He had ensured he was given assignments that allowed him to work in parts of the business that were expanding. He drove himself to work harder than his peers and had had good performance reviews. After two years when his traineeship was coming to an end, he asked for a conversation with his Manager. He told his Manager what he now expected, i.e. more responsibility, greater autonomy and a promotion within the year. His Manager asked him what made him believe that he would be ready for a promotion within a year. Henry talked about the commitment he had given, his willingness to learn and the contribution he felt he had made. His Manager then asked him what he thought the promoted post required. Henry was silent for a moment. He had not thought about the promotion in terms of what it required, he had thought of it in terms of what it represented to him, i.e. recognition of his efforts. He made a few vague statements before his Manager asked if he would like him to outline the key differences between his current post and the desired one. Henry said he would welcome more information. The Manager pointed out what would be required, and asked Henry how that looked to him. He quickly claimed he could see no problems for him, and asked when his Manager thought such a position would come up. Up to this point, his Manager had been offering information, but he now switched position, by asking if Henry would like some feedback on how he saw him against the demands of the position. Henry agreed that it would be helpful, and his Manager provided detailed feedback on where he saw the gap between Henry's current skills and the demands of the next level up. In getting that feedback, Henry was then able to define how to focus his development so that when such a post came up he would be well positioned. Without that feedback, Henry would have seen it as an entitlement for his efforts, and felt affronted if he had not got the post. It would have driven him to look for employment elsewhere, on the grounds that his efforts were not appreciated. With that feedback he learnt that promotion is not just a reward for past effort, but a recognition of the possession of skills that will be applied to the demands of the new role. His Manager was not discounting his previous efforts, but showing through his feedback that those skills were necessary but not sufficient for what he aspired to.

Feedback in the moment

There is one other form of reality expansion that a Manager can offer within a FAST coaching conversation, and that is feedback on what is happening in the moment. This feedback does not demand that you bring any knowledge from outside the situation, but that you feedback on what you see happening. It requires that you use your listening with intent skills to point out discrepancies between words and actions, words and emotions, the words of the mouth and the words of the body.

Examples

Coachee: I really want to get better at prioritizing.

Coach: You say that you want to prioritize, but you have just told me that you have not made time to do anything different since our last conversation.

Purpose of feedback
To test if prioritization is the real issue.

> *Coachee:* I don't mind about not getting the job.
>
> *Coach:* You looked down as you said that. I suspect you do mind.

Purpose of feedback
To show that you are open to them talking about their feelings of disappointment.

> *Coachee:* I am happy to fill in for them while they are away.
>
> *Coach:* You voice did not sound happy as you said it.

Purpose of feedback
To enable them to bring into the open their true feelings about an increased work load.

> *Coachee:* Because I have high expectations of myself, I expect a lot of other people.
>
> *Coach:* I feel those expectations on me when we talk. Would you like some feedback on how it feels?

Purpose of feedback
To enable them to see the impact of their behaviour on others, through the coach feeding back on their experience of the coachee within the coaching session.

The last example is an important one. The coach is not offering to give feedback on how they feel about the coachee generally. They are offering specific feedback on the impact they have on the coach in a coaching conversation. They do this because by giving feedback it will help the coachee better understand how others respond to them.

Giving feedback in the moment is also a way of not colluding with the coachee. Coachees can want to see the Manager Coach as a rescuer, as someone who will put right what is causing them difficulty. They will look for evidence that the Manager Coach will take their side, rather than being alongside. They will therefore send out requests for feedback that are, in reality, requests for support. It is important that, in giving feedback in the moment, that the Manager Coach is not hooked by that request.

EXAMPLE

Coachee: Losing that account, even though I did my best, makes me feel I have no chance of being given one of the major accounts this year? Do you think I have blown it? (*Request for support masquerading as request for feedback*)

Coach: Losing an account like that is significant. (*Reality feedback*)

Coachee: But it's not fair, no one worked harder than me to try and get it sorted.

Coachee: I saw how hard you worked, but it did not work out. (*Observational feedback and reality feedback*) What have you learnt from the experience that is useful to getting back on track?

CASE STUDY

Eva, asked her Manager for help in being more influential. She was a knowledge expert within her area, but complained that she felt her expertise was discounted, or that others claimed credit for her ideas months after she had first put them forward. As she explained in greater and greater detail the content of her current work and why she felt others should listen to it, her Manager Coach could feel himself disengaging from any interest in the topic. He took the risk of giving straight feedback. 'I notice that the more detail you give me, the less I listen, and I am wondering if it has the same effect on other people'. Eva grabbed at the feedback, confirming that she had noticed others disengaging, but did not know what to do when this happened. Her Manager Coach asked if she would like some more feedback, based on what he had noticed in their conversation so far. Eva accepted the invitation. He told Eva that he noticed that when she started talking about her subject area, it was as though there was no-one else in the room. She moved into a stream of consciousness that was difficult to interrupt and that did not seem intended to involve the other person. It was difficult to see what they were supposed to bring to the conversation, since it largely became a monologue.

This feedback was the starting point in Eva starting to develop strategies to bring the realities as seen by others into their discussions with her. She quickly found that when she made room for their thoughts alongside her own, she was able to take account of their views, flex her argument and achieve her purpose. The Manager took the risk of giving her feedback in the moment, from which she was able to start moving forward. Without that feedback, Eva was stuck in a self-justifying monologue, where she had all the knowledge and it was the fault of others that they could not see the value of it.

EXERCISE

The giving of feedback is one of the least developed skills in most managerial repertoires. Because of this it needs practice if it is to be used within a coaching conversation. Approach this exercise in stages.

Stage One

Notice when a member of staff does something really well. Rather than saying, 'That was great', ask if they would like any feedback on their work. If they accept the offer, then ask them what specifically they would like feedback on. Give that specific feedback. This may well not have been the feedback that would have occurred to you to offer. Because humans are self-critical, it is likely that even within a performance that you judge 'great' overall, there is something that they are less happy with. By asking them to identify it, you have the opportunity to either challenge their view of reality, or to confirm it.

Stage Two

In a discussion with a staff member, offer feedback in the moment. Feedback in the moment is short reality bites, e.g. 'I notice that ...', 'I sense that ...', 'I hear a discrepancy between ...'. Notice how the conversation is changed when you bring your feedback in the moment into your conversation.

Stage Three

Finally, raise the bar to offer a reality bite that confronts a reality that the other person is ignoring. When they complain, rationalize or discount a problem, make the offer of some feedback on the issue. Ask specifically what feedback would be useful to them, and offer it based on observation rather than judgement. Notice that the feedback they ask for may not be all that you could offer, but it will be heard if it is feedback against their purpose.

Notice what changes as a result of your feedback.

Summary

This chapter has used the principles of the Johari window to identify ways in which the coachee's area of known reality can be expanded through the intervention of the coach. It has used the frameworks of:

- Positional perspectives – to help the coachee move from a first-position view of reality to one that incorporates the perceptions of others.
- Seeking exceptions – to help the coachee move beyond the polarities of 'Never and Always' to find times when the problem is not present, and to identify what they do on those occasions.
- Offering feedback that is specific to the other's purpose based on non-judgemental observation.
- Offering feedback that arises in the moment of the conversation.

References

1. Luft, J. (1984) *Group Processes: An Introduction to Group Dynamics*. Third edition. Mayfield Publishing Company.
2. Grinder, J. and De Lozier, J. (1996) *Turtles All the Way Down: Prerequisites to Personal Growth*. Metamorphous Press.
3. O'Connor, J. and Lages, A. (2004) *Coaching with NLP*. Element.
4. de Jong, P. and Berg, I.K. (2002) *Interviewing for Solutions*. Brooks Cole, p. 104.

9

Targeting

The road leading you to a goal does not separate you from the destination,
it is essentially a part of it.
Charles de Lint

Most books on coaching start from the position that it is the setting of the goal that is the catalyst to change. Define the goal at the outset and then identify what is available to help the goal be achieved. It is an approach with a long pedigree. Aristotle, writing in the 3rd century BC, said 'First, have a definite, clear practical ideal; a goal, an objective. Second, have the necessary means to achieve your ends; wisdom, money, materials, and methods. Third, adjust all your means to that ends'. It seems a logical approach, and it is one that is followed every day in business. This book has taken a different approach. In Set Up, we began not with defining the goal, but with agreeing the purpose of the conversation. The difference between the two is important. Goal setting suggests clarity about what is wanted, and often individuals dealing with work performance or personal development issues are not clear about what they want. They are clearer about what is making them dissatisfied or unhappy, demotivated or lacking in confidence. Alternately, they are quick to identify a goal because they understand that is what is expected. However, the goal may be a flawed one. It may focus on the wrong area or it may be stated simply because it is thought to be acceptable to the listener. To start with a stated goal can lead to wasted time, as the individual is driven to commit too early to something of which they do not fully understand the consequences. The conversation may be short, but if the goal is not on target, committed action will not follow. Manager Coaches need coaching conversations to be FAST. Paradoxically, this means holding off from goal setting until the coachee is clear on what they want to achieve.

I place goal setting not as the start of the conversation, but as the culmination of the second stage of the conversation. In Stage I, we set up the conditions for a helping conversation, through the listening and rapport-building skills of the Manager Coach that allow the staff member to talk openly. From this the purpose of the conversation is agreed. In Stage II, the staff member is helped to define the tangibles of the situation, to explore the assumptions surrounding it, and to get multiple perspectives alongside their view of reality.

Their knowledge about themselves has been expanded through the skills used by the Manager Coach to the point where the individual is much better equipped to choose their true goal. In the words of Kofi Annan, Secretary General of the UN, 'To live is to choose. But to choose well, you must know who you are and what you stand for, where you want to go and why you want to get there'.[1] In the second phase of the conversation, the skill of the coach is to support the coachee in accessing knowledge and insights that were not previously available to them, through the questions posed and the challenge to thought they provide. With those new sources of information, the coachee is now ready to start defining goals with which they strongly identify, which motivate them and where they have skills that can be applied to their achievement.

The end of the second stage of the coaching conversation is reached when the Manager Coach sees and hears in the coachee's reaction that they have said enough to define what it is they really want to be different. This can happen after establishing the tangibles of the situation, it may happen once they have challenged their own assumptions or you may recognize it in offering a challenge to their view of reality. There will be an 'aha!' moment when what they need to do becomes clear to them. Alternatively, the question 'What else?' has no further reply. They signal 'No, that's it', in a way that shows they are satisfied with the point they have reached. As a coach all you need do at this point is to ask the question that brings closure to Stage II and opens up Stage III.

The question: *Now what is it you want to do?*

The question is an invitation to state a goal, but a goal that is rooted in the important aspects that have emerged from the conversation. What has emerged can be very different from where the conversation began. It is a question that always brings a response and a response that defines the next stage.

Some years ago, an accountant came to see me in the Art School where I then worked. He stated from the beginning that his goal was to become a painter, since from his perspective being an accountant was a well-paid but pointless activity. Impressed by his clarity, I initially saw it as an invitation to explain the entry procedures for mature students, knowing that mature students were successful because of their motivation. I stopped myself, and started to explore some of the tangibles about his stated goal. In doing so I quickly learnt that he had done a little painting on weekend courses, and enjoyed art exhibitions. He was very taken with the work of Gauguin, and inspired by his life story as a stockbroker who had abandoned a conventional life to paint. I checked out his assumptions about the life of a painter, and what he believed it would give him: freedom, fun, self-expression, relationships with creative women; and I reality checked through asking him to identify what he would give up in becoming a painter. The last question stopped him in his tracks. He had not thought of painting as involving giving up anything, but rather as an opening up of himself. I showed him the career outcomes and income levels I held on graduates of the Fine Art Department and he became quiet. In his perception of reality, becoming an artist was visual 'rock 'n' roll', with the unspoken assumption that he would be one of its stars. It did not equate with the hand to mouth existence that was described in the statistics. A silence then followed, before I asked him, 'Now what is it you want to do?'. He replied, 'I want to find a way as an accountant of working with artists'.

He could never have claimed that goal at the outset, because it would have felt like a cop-out. Had I simply gone with his stated goal, I could have propelled him into something he had not fully thought through. By holding back from the goal until the context had been fully explored, a goal emerged that motivated him. He wanted to be around artists and to experience a culture different from that of his profession, but he did not want the lifestyle implications of that choice.

An approach that puts goal setting as a mid-point process does not fit with the conventional target-focused approach, which sees the goal as the kick-off point. The difference in this approach is that all the Stage II energy is directed towards defining the right goal.

CASE STUDY

Pippa, a high-energy Sales Manager, had difficulties with her Sales Director. He was highly directive and controlling, and Pippa was the latest in a long line of young sales staff who had come in with enthusiasm and had ultimately left because of him. Pippa asked for a coaching session wanting to find a way of getting the Sales Director to change. The coach pointed out that it was impossible to set a goal that involved a behaviour change for another person, but was there an alternative purpose that the conversation could serve. Pippa, eventually said that just to talk about the Sales Director and how she dealt with him would be helpful. The purpose at the outset was simply to talk about her relationship with the Sales Director. This could have been an opportunity to moan but the coach, having offered support for Pippa's thinking, then encouraged her to identify tangibles about when the difficulties occurred and when the difficulties did not occur. The coach looked to build some content about the relationship, rather than relying only on feelings. In doing this, Pippa recognized that when she stood her ground and backed it up with hard data the Sales Director did respond. He failed to respond when Pippa talked about ideas and future possibilities, unconnected with present realities. The coach then probed her on her assumptions about the Sales Director, and quickly unearthed that Pippa assumed the Sales Director was a misogynist, incapable of recognizing the contribution of a young woman. The challenge to check out whether the assumption was true prompted her to acknowledge that gender played little part in his behaviours. He was as likely to be rude towards a male counterpart. Asked to consider how the Sales Director would see their relationship, she saw that he viewed her as full of enthusiasm, but quickly bored. She saw that from his perspective she started things off but did not finish them before wanting to go on to the next thing.

With these insights, the coach asked Pippa the closure question, 'Now what is it you want to do?' *(invitation to state a goal)*.

Pippa replied, 'I want to do a piece of work that shows that I can deal with the detail, and can stick with it until the end' *(goal identified)*.

The rest of the session then focused on defining the piece of work and action planning how they would achieve it.

In defining the goal, a shift had occurred. The focus was not the Sales Director but on what Pippa could do that would make her more effective, regardless of who her Sales Director was. The hope is that in delivering on the goal that has taken account of the Sales Director's view of reality, Pippa will become more impactful with him. Even if the Sales Director proves intransigent, Pippa will have developed a new way of working that will serve her well, whoever she works for.

In taking the time to challenge and support thinking in Stage II of the conversation, there are many and diverse goals that can emerge. In looking at the relationship with the Sales Director she could have answered the question 'Now what is it you want to do?' in many ways:

- 'I want to leave'
- 'I want to have a conversation with him where I explain the impact of his style on me'
- 'I want to get him to help me develop a more business focused approach'
- 'I want to achieve my best sales figures ever so that my approach is vindicated'.

There is no right or better goal. The role of the coach is to help the coachee reach the point where they can define a goal that moves them beyond the point at which they entered the conversation and that is meaningful for them. As the coach, this may not be the goal you would choose, but it is the right goal for the other person at that time.

The challenge for the Manager Coach is to be detached and to have no emotional investment in one goal being better than any other. This can be hard, particularly when you have a line responsibility. It asks that you stay in the moment with the coachee, and not bring into their space your competing goal.

SAMPLE DIALOGUE

Coachee: Now that you have helped me to think things through I am seeing things differently.

Coach: I am glad. Now what is it you want to do?

Coachee: I can see now that what I want to do is to move into another department, to get the sort of experience I am missing.

Coach: Are you sure that is a good idea?

Coachee: You don't think it is?

Coach: Well, I don't think it's great timing given everything we have to deliver on in the next half year.

> *Coachee:* Oh so what do you think I should do?
>
> *Coach:* I think you need to think about the impact on me of moving out in the next few months.
>
> *Coachee:* I thought we were looking at what was right for me. I am obviously not going to do anything rash that will make things difficult for you and the rest of the department.

The agenda has switched in three exchanges, from gratitude for help in identifying a motivating and relevant goal, to resentment directed towards the coach for switching the focus of attention.

As a Manager Coach you will have concerns but they have to be set aside for as long as you are offering yourself as a coach. If you are not able at this point to remain dispassionate, you need to signal that clearly.

> *Coachee:* Now that you have helped me to think things through I am seeing things differently.
>
> *Coach:* I am glad. Now what is it you want to do?
>
> *Coachee:* I can see now that what I want to do is to move into another department, to get the sort of experience I am missing.
>
> *Coach:* Do you have a sense of which department would provide that experience?
>
> *Coachee:* I am not sure, I need to go and have a conversation with HR to try and understand what is going on elsewhere in the business.
>
> *Coach:* When do you think you could do that?
>
> *Coachee:* Well, I am really busy right now, so I guess it won't be until after the next quarterly results meeting.
>
> *Coach:* OK, well I would like you to get back to me on what comes out of that conversation. I obviously have an interest in the outcome, and its implications for meeting objectives.
>
> *Coachee:* Of course, I am not going to do anything without keeping you in the loop and discussing it with you. I don't want to create difficulties.

In the second conversation, the coach, by keeping themselves out of the focus and continuing to signal that they are there to support the other's thinking, allows the coachee to access their own sense of responsibility, rather than having it imposed on them. The coachee recognizes that the coach is also their manager, and retains the sense of gratitude that the coach was willing to work with them.

The question, 'Now what is it you want to do?' is a deliberate question. It acknowledges the coachee's perspective may well have changed as a result of being given both support and challenge. It shows that it is acceptable to have a very different agenda from that they initially brought to the conversation. It also signals that the definition of the goal is the starting point for moving towards action. It is a sign that the support and challenge that the coach has made available for thinking is now going to be used in supporting and challenging them to act.

There is a final value in asking 'Now what do you want to do?'. It may be that the process of exploration has not defined the goal, but it has highlighted that the original purpose was not accurate. Asking the question allows for the coachee to return to the beginning of the process, but with the insights that have come from their work so far. Asking a coachee what they want to do, asked from an open spirit of enquiry rather than an implied directive to get on and do something, gives them permission to tell you that they need to do some more thinking, if your skilful questioning has helped them realize that their original purpose was faulty.

EXAMPLE

A coachee has come to a session saying that they are having problems with a colleague, and that they feel they are being taken advantage of because they are reluctant to get involved in conflict. They state that their purpose is to look at ways in which they could influence that colleague. The Manager Coach allows them to talk about a number of situations in which they have held back from expressing their opinion, and then gone away feeling demeaned. The coach also helps them to identify a time when they have worked well with the colleague, which has allowed them to recognize that the relationship is not difficult all the time. The coach encourages them to consider how their behaviour looks from the perspective of the colleague, and they acknowledge that for that colleague they are probably an unknown quantity, since they bring out into the open so little of their thoughts and feelings. The Manager Coach asks what a supportive colleague of theirs would notice about them, and they say, 'That I am inscrutable, even when things are going badly'. The coach asks the 'what else?' question a couple of times, and the coachee eventually says, 'There's nothing else'. The coach then asks, 'Now what do you want to do?', and they reply, 'I want to find a way of bringing what I am thinking and feeling into the open'.

This is less a goal than a new definition of purpose. Before it can become a goal that can be acted on it needs a context. The conversation has unearthed that this is more than an issue with one individual, it is a trait that impacts on how the coachee deals with other people. The coach now knows that they need to go around the second stage again to collect additional data, looking for resources that will help once the true goal has been defined, and challenging the assumptions held about the risks of bringing their thoughts and feelings to the attention of others. Going around the cycle again means that when the goal is defined it will have an engaging clarity for the coachee. They will have discovered that there are positive assumptions that will support them in their goal, and they will have identified when and where they want to apply this trait. The goal in its final form may look very different from their initial opening, but they will know it is the right goal.

CASE STUDY

Eric had been invited to join a start-up dot.com headed by a charismatic businesswoman. Eric greatly admired her, her skills and her energy, and he sought her approval. As the business was young, it had a roller-coaster existence. There was always too much work and never enough resource, and Eric had become swept up in doing more and more. He came to the coaching process exhausted. He was working sixteen-hour days and yet still felt he was failing. He stated his purpose as wanting to find a way of not feeling responsible for everything. He had a well-understood pattern of being the responsible one that he linked with his childhood. Being the eldest son in a single-parent family, he had learnt from a young age that it was important not to shirk responsibility, in order to be seen as a good son. He understood his problem, and it was easy for him to talk about it but this did not help him do things differently. Instead of looking further at the problem, since recognizing it did not produce solutions, the coach asked him to look at his behaviour from the perspective of his CEO – what did he see?

From this position Eric saw that the CEO saw someone who constantly said 'Yes', and then could not deliver fully. He saw someone who did not seem to have a sense of priorities and who found it difficult to see what his real added value was. The coach asked Eric to look at himself from the perspective of the business. From this perspective Eric saw that the business would get more if he offered less. What would benefit the business was bringing his distinct skills to bear, rather than trying to show that he was a 'Jack of all Trades'.

When the coach, asked the 'Now what do you want to do?' question, Eric replied that he wanted to get a clear sense of what his real strengths were so that he could present them as a positive offering to the business, and use that offer to define the boundaries of what he should take responsibility for.

With this new purpose the coach was able to ask questions that helped Eric define times when he had given his best performance, and had experienced a sense of being valued by others. The database he generated meant that when the 'Now what do you want to do?' question was asked again, he was able to state a goal: to prepare for a meeting where he could re-negotiate his role based on what he could best bring to the business.

Once the purposeful goal has been defined as the end point of Stage II, the bulk of the work of the coaching session has been done – the top of the hill has been reached. From that vantage point the coachee can now see so much further, and the destination they are wanting to reach is clearly visible. They can now start moving quickly towards that destination, drawing on their own resources. The task of the Manager Coach switches from helping their thinking so that resources are found, to helping them apply the right resources to achieve their goal.

Summary

In this chapter, we have come to the beginning of Stage III of the FAST coaching conversation. That stage comes when the coach is confident that the coachee has explored the situation to the point where a motivating goal has emerged.

- The goal setting point comes when the next obvious question is 'Now what do you want to do?'.

- The goal that emerges does not have to be the best goal. It will not be the only possible goal, but it is the goal that is right for that person at that time.
- The challenge for the Manager Coach is being able to stay working for the coachee even if the goal has implications for them.
- Where the purpose of the conversation changes as a result of the questioning skills of the Manager Coach, the 'Now what do you want to do?' question allows the coachee to revisit their purpose and start again.
- Holding back from goal setting until the coachee is ready to define an appropriate motivating goal supports FAST coaching, rather than slowing it down.

References

1. ThinkExist.com Quotations Online 1 July 2005. http://en.thinkexist.com/quotes/kofi_annan/.

10

Emerging solutions

Always be on the lookout for ways to turn a problem into an
opportunity for success.
Lao Tzu

Even a little progress is complete freedom from fear.
Bhagavad Gita

Coaching provides space for exploration so that the right goal can emerge, the solutions to enable the goal are identified, and the resources to be applied in their achievement are found. This chapter is concerned with supporting the process of building solutions. It is an exciting stage. A stage that has an ease to it, provided that:

- The right target for that individual is found.
- The right amount of stretch for that individual is defined.
- The right resources from that individual's experience pool are applied.

It is a stage at which the Manager Coach is offering support for thought, through offering frameworks to help the process of solution-finding. It is the time when all the hard work that the Manager Coach has done in Stages I and II reaps its rewards. When that work has been done well, any anxiety that the coach had at the beginning of the conversation that they will be expected to produce answers disappears, since it becomes clear that the coachee is able to, and wants to, produce their own solutions. The Manager Coach can enjoy the momentum of cruising downhill; still mindful of their role but feeling comfortable that the coachee is in control.

The need now is to hone the coachee's thinking through helping them to establish what needs to be different if their goal is to be achieved, and what they have available to them that will make that difference.

The quality of the work done in Stage II can make the solution-finding process effortless. Having recognized their target, what needs to be done to achieve it flows automatically, drawing on the insights the coachee has gained from the earlier stages of the conversation.

The Manager Coach is helped, however, by having some tools available to structure thinking on solution finding. One of the most useful of these is scaling.

Scaling

Scaling is a deceptively simple technique, developed in Solution Focused Therapy.[1,2] Its value is that it allows people to easily express complex thoughts about their past experience and their future possibilities; thoughts from which solutions are found. Its power is that it is possible to create a scale around any goal that an individual creates. Its gift is that the scale is entirely in the hands of the coachee; it demands nothing of the Manager Coach other than creating the opportunity for the coachee to work with their scale.

EXAMPLE

An individual has brought to the coaching conversation their difficulty with a member of staff. That person is able, at the end of Stage II of the conversation, to answer the question, 'Now what do you want to do?' with the response, 'I want to confront their poor performance'. Given that they have probably known this for some time, it is not the goal that is the insight, it is acknowledging that they are committing to taking action, and that in order to do so they need confidence.

Stating of the goal opens up the opportunity to create a scale, through inviting the coachee to create a measure around the chances of them confronting their poor performer.

Scales are usually 0–10. The polarities are, however, defined by the coachee.

One individual may decide:
0 = could not even contemplate confronting them
10 = confronting them with confidence.

Another individual facing the same issue may decide:
0 = confronting so ineptly that things get worse
10 = confronting so skilfully that the relationship improves.

0   10

Figure 10.1 The starting scale

A third may define the polarities as:

0 = avoiding confrontation in the expectation of failure

10 = confronting without worrying about controlling the outcome.

For a scale to be of value in supporting the emergence of solutions, the polarities are in the ownership of the coachee. In this instance the coachee defines the scale as:

0 = could not imagine confronting their poor performance

10 = confronting poor performance as soon as I notice it.

Challenge for the Manager Coach

As a coach this means accepting that the coachee's polarities may well not be your polarities. The Manager Coach who intervenes in the process through deciding what the polarities should be derails the exercise. Having decided on meaningful polarities, the coachee is then invited to rate their present performance against that scale. In this instance, the individual rates themselves at 2.

Challenge for the Manager Coach

From your perspective, this may seem an inappropriate rating. You may see them as regularly confronting situations, and feel that they are underselling themselves. You may be a 'cup-half-full person', who cannot understand how anyone would rate themselves so low, and have an urge to encourage a higher rating. Alternately, they may rate themselves at 8, a rating with which you profoundly disagree, based on your experience of them. The challenge for the coach is to accept that this is their perception, and it is from this that you are helping them build solutions.

A rating of 2 may appear that there is little to work with, but solution focused coaching looks for what is there, and asks the individual to explain what 2 looks like. What are they doing that explains rating themselves at 2 rather than 0?

Their first reply is likely to be in the negative:

- Well I know they will resist the minute I try and give them tough feedback.
- I lose confidence when I can see their body language stiffen up.

Challenge for the Manager Coach

The challenge for the coach is to keep the other person focused on the resources that are there, even in a rating of 2. Since they have not rated themselves at 0, what it is it that they are doing, as distinct from not doing? They may reply:

- I did once manage to get him/her to listen to a difficult message.
- I believe it is too important to ignore.
- I have got some time with them next week, and I have flagged up that piece of work as something I want to talk about.

Someone who sees themselves as failing in an area of their work ignores contrary evidence. The coach's role is to help them find that evidence, no matter how small.

A common fear is that the coachee will place themselves as 0. In reality, this rarely, if ever, happens. Even if it does, it allows for getting negative data into the open on what specifically contributes to a rating of 0. The Manager Coach can accept their assessment, knowing that the next question forces a shift in thinking.

The question:

Where do you think you need to be in order to . . .?

invites the coachee to identify the place on the scale that they aspire to. The point at which they can achieve their goal. At this point it becomes untenable to remain at 0, since change is impossible from this position. The answer will come at any point beyond their present rating, and it may not be 10.

Challenge for the Manager Coach

This is another point at which the urge to intervene can be strong. Goal achievement suggests that individuals should be aspiring to 10. However, from the other's perspective this may be beyond their present reach. Solution focused coaching looks to create and build on progress, however small, since it is from a sense of progress that bigger goals emerge. Solution building does not demand that the individual sets themselves a goal that, at that moment, seems unachievable.

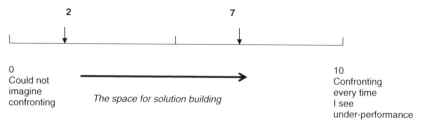

Figure 10.2   Space for solution building

This coachee identifies 7 as the point they would like to reach. Although a number has no absolute meaning, it will have meaning for them. That meaning is revealed through asking the question:

What would be different if you were at 7?

This simple question invites the other person to start identifying the data they are looking for that will signal the desired change has happened. They answer:

- I would have performance data to hand when we speak, rather than relying on my impressions.
- I would own what I am saying, rather than saying, 'people tell me that you are not ...'.
- I would clear my diary for 30 minutes before meeting with them, so that I prepare my argument and anticipate their objections.
- I would write down key phrases to keep me focused when they start trying to deflect me.
- I would keep in mind the reason I am challenging their performance, rather than worrying about myself.

In identifying the difference, it is apparent in their answers that they have identified their solutions.

Challenge for the Manager Coach

Once they have identified the differences, the challenge for the Manager Coach is to help them find evidence that they have applied those solutions before, so that the implementation of the solution becomes easier. The evidence may already be there. In talking through the issue, reality bite questioning could have allowed them to recognize that exceptionally they do many of those things they are now seeking to apply to this situation. In this case, the Manager Coach simply needs to remind them of the resource. If that evidence has not emerged, the coach supports them through questioning to seek out exceptions, or to test out the difficulty of doing something they have not previously done.

If it becomes clear that the individual has never applied any of the solutions that they are now looking to use, the Manager Coach can help them rescale their aspirations, through asking them to define:

What would one point up from where you currently are look like?

Looking one point up provides solutions that are easily achieved, and from which a sense of progress can build. This is important when the scale of aspiration is larger than the resources available. One point up in this instance could be:

- 'Making a few phone calls to internal customers to get some feedback data. It would give me some backbone knowing it is not just me who thinks this.'
- 'Getting out their objectives and using them in our weekly meeting to signal that I have my eye on performance delivery.'
- 'Extracting data from the Management Information System so that I know I have some objective information on their performance.'

Any one of these 'one point ups' will provide a basis for moving up to the next point, and from this identifying the next scale point.

Challenge for the Manager Coach

The challenge for the Manager Coach is to hold back from giving solutions. You will see many other things that they could do, but their ownership will be much greater for those things they identify themselves. It also asks that the Manager Coach accepts that there are many routes to the same destination. While the route the coachee takes may not be your route, if it gets them to the right place they do not need your map.

Sometimes, the individual will signal that they recognize the gap, but that they are struggling with how to make the difference. In this case, it can be helpful to *ask* if they would like some suggestions to get their thinking moving. This is qualitatively different from telling them what they should do. The purpose in making suggestions is not to signal your superior knowledge or experience, but to pump-prime their thinking. A suggestion is a pebble thrown in order to stir up the surface of the other's thoughts, rather than to provide the answer. In making the suggestion, the Manager Coach has to be prepared for it to be rejected, accepting that its value is in helping them clarify their own solutions.

Because a scale is a simple visual structure that allows for framing sometimes complex thoughts, it speeds up the solution-building process. The process of putting things on a scale allows for expressing subjective thoughts and feelings within a structure that accepts them as objective. Its strength lies in the fact that it can be applied to any target that has been identified:

Target:
The confidence to speak out in a large meeting.
Scale: confidence in large groups.

Target:
To influence a US project worker when contact is only by telephone.
Scale: ability to influence at a distance.

Target:
To gain a promotion through committing 110 per cent to work over the next year.
Scale: willingness to commit 110 per cent.

Target:
To find a way of working with the organizational changes rather than resisting them.
Scale: willingness to change.

Target:
To delegate more to direct reports.
Scale: comfort in delegating.

CASE STUDY

Vanessa had had an early career as a university lecturer. She joined a multinational in her late 20s and worked in a series of jobs where her analytical abilities, retention of detail and ability to see to the heart of an issue quickly brought her recognition. Being intelligent marked her out until she found herself on a subsidiary board of the company, working alongside an equally able peer group. They quickly came to resent her style. She was too quick to provide answers to others' problems and could not understand why they were not grateful for her incisiveness. She felt that they thought she did it out of a sense of competition, when from her viewpoint it was simply instinctive.

Through coaching she came to recognize that her target was to use her intelligence corporately to help support others' thinking, rather than to display her own.

Her coach invited her to create a scale around her cleverness. She created a scale:

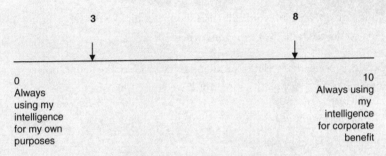

Figure 10.3 Vanessa's scale

On this scale, 3 represented current reality. She sensed that her inputs were occasionally welcomed, and she knew that sometimes she held back and did not say all that she wanted to say. Vanessa's intentions were good, but her ability to sustain a corporate perspective fell away when the debate was intense.

At 8 she recognized that the difference would be created by:

- Going through the agenda and planning her contributions, not on what excited her but on the degree to which they were intended to address a corporate need.
- Developing criteria for her interventions.
- Looking to build on others' ideas rather than demolishing them.
- Asking for feedback from the Chair on her behaviour in board meetings, by sharing with him what she was trying to achieve.

Vanessa recognized that this way of behaving was not an easy one for her. To have set a target of 10 would have allowed her to let herself off the hook by seeing it as unattainable. By working towards 8 she was committing to doing things differently. She never did get to 10 but, by showing that she was working hard on making a shift in how she interacted with colleagues, her colleagues became more accepting of the times when the desire to be the cleverest girl in the class overwhelmed her.

Scaling is a powerful means of helping an individual to define those things they can do differently to achieve the degree of change that will motivate their efforts.

EXERCISE

Think of an area of your life that you would like to set a target for. This could relate to work or your wider life roles.

Create a scale that relates to that target, and define your polarities – remembering that polarities do not have to be opposites.

Your personal scale

0   10

Figure 10.4 Your personal scale

On the scale mark the point that represents your present performance against the scale.

Identify what contributes to that rating. What are you doing (as distinct from not doing) that explains your assessment?

Then identify the point where you wish to be against your target. This does not have to be 10.

What is the difference that sits in the space between your present and your desired rating?

What would one point up from your present rating look like?

Review what emerges from the scaling process that is helpful to your attaining your target.

What solutions have you identified?

The Miracle Question

An alternate means of unearthing the desired changes is through the use of the ultimate quantum question: the Miracle Question.

Organizations do not deal in miracles, but the power of the question is that it encourages the individual to imagine that the target has been achieved, and to identify the evidence of the change that will be visible. The wording of the question, derived from the work of Steve de Shazer,[3] is intentionally dramatic.

Suppose that while you were asleep tonight, a miracle happens. The miracle is that the problem we have talked about is solved. Because you have been asleep, you don't know that the miracle has happened. So when you walk into work, what will you notice that will tell you that the miracle has occurred?

Challenge for the Manager Coach

The challenge for the Manager Coach is that it requires confidence to talk of miracles in an organizational setting. Miracles are the provenance of those aspiring to sainthood, not the behaviour of ordinary, flawed individuals simply doing their job. The purpose behind the question is not related to an expectation that a problem will be removed by a miracle, but as an enabler to identifying what the coachee is looking to change in concrete terms. It is a tactic to encourage the individual to stand above the problem and to identify the range of small changes that would contribute to the target being achieved rather than seeing change as coming as a complete whole. It also encourages thinking about how the change would be recognized, not just by themselves but by the network of people who have an interest in their desired change.

SAMPLE DIALOGUE

A direct report brings the issue of their inability to supervise a member of their team, who is a good friend outside of work. They find themselves constantly hooked by not wanting to endanger their friendship, which leads them to tolerate behaviour they would not accept in others. They recognize that others in the team notice this and it is making them lose respect. In answer to the question, 'Now what do you want to do?' they reply:

Coachee: I want to find a way of holding onto a sense of being a responsible supervisor first and not a friend first.

Coach: That's clear. Now I am going to ask you a question that may seem strange. I want you to imagine that while you are asleep, a miracle happens. You become the responsible supervisor that you want to be. But, because this happens while you are asleep you don't know it has happened. When you come into work tomorrow, what will be the first things that you notice that tell you that the miracle has taken place?

Coachee: I don't believe in miracles. It's not going to happen that way.

Coach: You don't have to believe in miracles, I just want you to tell me what you would notice that would tell you that your problem has been removed.

Coachee: Well it would be miraculous if I came in and I wasn't thinking, 'I wonder if this will be OK for him?'.

Coach: So you would notice that you were not wondering about how they would react to any decisions you make, as your starting point.
What do you notice about your first thoughts as you sit at your desk?

Coachee: I am focusing on what we have got to achieve as a team.

Coach: You are seeing the whole team and not just him. What else?

Coachee: I notice that when I look at his work, I am looking at it objectively, rather than looking at it in the hope that there is nothing there that I should pick up on.

Coach: What are you doing instead?

Coachee: I am talking with him about how he approached a piece of work, and offering feedback to improve it. I am giving him positives, but I am not afraid to also challenge his thoughts if I think they will improve the outcome.

> *Coach:* What is your friend noticing?
>
> *Coachee:* He notices that I am being more serious and that I am not deflected by his jokes.
>
> *Coach:* Anything you notice about yourself?
>
> *Coachee:* I look OK because I am not feeling uncomfortable. What I am saying doesn't mean we can't be friends, it is saying when we work together, we have to behave differently.
>
> *Coach:* And what would someone in your team notice?
>
> *Coachee:* They would see that I am smiling less but that my smiles are more relaxed. They would notice that I am spending more time with them.

The Miracle Question is powerful because it invites the other person to create a possible future. As they talk they are talking as though the change has happened, and in doing so they have identified what they can do in order to make that change happen. The question does not suggest that the problem will be removed with a wave of a wand, but in the changes they notice are the signals of what they want to do differently, and the positive consequences of those changes.

The challenge for the Manager Coach

The first challenge is to ask the question with confidence. If the coach signals their discomfort with the question, or shows by a facial gesture that they think it is 'off the wall', the coachee will take their cue from them, and dismiss it. If the Manager Coach asks it confidently, and in a spirit of genuine interest because they have a clear sense of why it is helpful to finding solutions, the coachee will follow their lead.

Even if they do follow that lead, since they do not understand the underlying purpose of the question the coachee is likely to start with vague responses. It is their way of protecting themselves from revealing too much. It is here that the Manager Coach needs to stay with the line of questioning, encouraging them to talk in detail so that the conversation becomes concrete. This solidity is increased by asking them to take a 360-degree perspective on the question. 'What do you notice?' 'What do the other protagonists notice?' In moving around the stakeholder system, the Manager Coach is modelling that any change they make will be noticed by and will influence the rest of the system. If the supervisor stops being deflected by jokes, their friend will stop telling them. If they start giving balanced feedback their friend will start looking at their work differently. If they start giving more time to the rest of the team, the team will start to shift their perspective on the supervisor. In the process of experiencing a different relationship with the team, the supervisor will be changed in how they view themselves, their relationship with their friend and the team. It enables the coachee to see that the payoff for change goes wider than the particulars of one situation.

The outcome of the Miracle Question is detailed information that becomes available to support the achievement of the stated target of being a responsible supervisor, rather than a friend first. It is now evident what the supervisor wants to experience differently, and they have gained a glimpse of how different things will be when they achieve it.

The coach can now use their tool kit to help them find the means of effecting those changes.

They may look for exceptions:

- Can you think of a time recently when you have been a responsible supervisor rather than a friend? When was it?
- What did you do? How did you do it? What was the effect?

They may offer the provocation:

- Always a friend first? As a means of helping them break out of the polarity they have set up regarding their relationship.

They may invite them to create a scale on responsible supervision:

- Asking them to define a dimension that is helpful, e.g. confidence, will, skill. In doing so they will be able to define the degree of shift they are looking for. Following on from the Miracle Question they are likely to look for a bigger shift than they would have done initially, because they have had sight of what the rewards could be of making a change.

They may invite them to identify the easiest thing they could imagine doing that would start the process moving, as a way of experiencing an early win from which they can build.

Challenge for the Manager Coach

Whatever information the Miracle Question produces is an opening for solution building. However, if, despite their best endeavours, the Manager Coach is met by complete resistance, a different tack is available. The coachee who 'does not do miracles', can still benefit from the motivation that comes from seeing a different future, through asking the question in a different way:

What will be different for you when the problem of . . . is solved?

What will tell you that . . . is no longer a problem?

If I were to see you in a month's time and you had dealt with this problem, what would I see you doing differently?

Each question allows for building the individual's preferred future view of the issue, and then expanding the angle of attention through drawing in the perspectives of the other stakeholders.

What will be different for your staff when . . . is no longer a problem for you?

What will tell your peers that . . . is no longer a problem for you?

If I were to ask . . . in a month's time when you have dealt with the problem, what would they see you doing differently?

There is no one question that will work for everyone. The skill of the Manager Coach is in keeping the coachee's intention in mind, and then honing their question to match with the style of each individual.

For individuals who have lived with an issue for some while, the possibility of the problem being removed may be beyond their imagination. In which case the question moves one step back and asks instead for evidence of improvement rather than resolution.

What would be a first sign for you that the problem is reducing in its impact?

What would be a first sign for others that the problem is beginning to be resolved?

No matter how small the belief that change is possible, the coach works to find it; because in holding up the possibility for the coachee's attention, they support them in finding a way forward.

CASE STUDY

Carl had left school at 16, started at the bottom of the organization and, by dint of hard work, had worked his way to Senior Management in a property development company. He had a fierce loyalty to the organization that had made him and, since the organization had been parental to him in his early years, he had made himself into a parental figure. The parental figure that he had become loved to develop his staff, was sensitive to others' needs, took on work rather than ask others to do it and was closely involved in the lives of his staff. He was much loved and respected, but he was also exhausted and, as he got older, his coping strategy of working longer hours than anyone else was becoming less sustainable. With coaching he came to see that his target was to do those things where he added value, rather than wanting to be valued for everything he did.

In answering the Miracle Question, he noticed that the next day when he came into work he had more time available because he was not answering questions that others brought to him largely to save their own efforts. He noticed that he was looking at papers that related to corporate issues, rather than looking over the work of others. He noticed that he felt less snappy because his time was not being eaten into all the time. He noticed that he walked around the building and dropped in to see colleagues rather than communicating by email because he felt far less time-pressured. He noticed that he made more demands on others to provide him with input to his agenda, rather than being used up supporting others' agendas. He also noticed that individuals were a bit taken aback by his new style, and were not entirely happy. His coach recognized that this observation was a covert way of expressing his own anxieties about becoming the person he was describing, so they stepped back. The canvas Carl was painting was too far ahead of what he could imagine being. The coach reduced the size of the miracle by asking him 'What would be a first sign for you that the problem is reducing?'. Carl stated that only having in his briefcase work that related directly to his responsibilities would be a sign to him that things were changing.

Asked to look for a sign that others around him would notice, he recognized that if he asked others to attend external networking meetings that were not commensurate with his level, others would notice, as he often attended events in order to make life easier for those with family responsibilities.

Solutions of this size were seen as achievable by Carl. Having succeeded at them, he was then able to raise the bar to bring more of the miracle into view. Only when he experienced the rewards that came from small-scale solutions, was he able to take the risk of increasing the size of his actions.

Building commitment to solutions

Finding solutions is motivating, but identifying a solution will not guarantee that it is applied. Finding the resources to apply to the solution through looking for exceptions does not guarantee they will be transferred across. Just as written evidence that an employee possesses a skill does not guarantee it will be applied at work. Sitting between ability and its application is the intervening variable of motivation. The role of the Manager Coach goes beyond supporting the other's thoughts in finding solutions to help achieve their target. It extends to helping the other person find the motivation to take risks, to do things differently, and to risk failure.

Success in effecting change is determined by the strength of motivation an individual brings to their goal. The coach has a role in helping the individual identify what motivations they can call on to help their resolve. The best way of doing this is through getting an understanding of what the target means for the coachee.

There are two questions that can help this process:

When you achieve this goal, what will it mean for you?

When you get this goal, what will it get you?

The first question is more often used. It allows the individual to identify internal rewards that will come from achievement:

- Self-confidence.
- Affirmation.

- That I am more than I thought I was.
- It will prove that I am not a failure.
- It will show I can control my own fate.

These are laudable meanings and, for some staff, this will be enough to anchor their sense of commitment. The belief that stretching ourselves will enhance our own sense of self is a powerful one. It is implicit in seven times *Tour de France* winner Lance Armstrong's autobiography title, *It's Not About the Bike*. The target may have been to be the greatest *Tour de France* cyclist, but the motivation came from a tough childhood and his experience of surviving cancer in his early 20s. In winning those races, he was validating himself at a level beyond his physical fitness or skill as a tactician.

The second question allows for a different response. Asking, 'What will getting a goal get you?', allows for articulating different kinds of responses:

- A promotion.
- My parent's approval.
- More money.
- Visibility.
- Better projects.
- A legacy.

It allows for an individual to acknowledge that the rewards that may really drive their commitment are external and tangible. It does not prevent them claiming the internal rewards, but it gives them permission to claim those externals when they are stronger drivers.

CASE STUDY

Hugh had trained as a lawyer and purposely targeted high-profile city firms for employment. He worked hard, putting in the hours that were demanded, in the expectation of reaching Partner. He didn't. In his mid-30s he was earning a six-figure salary and was feeling a failure. When a friend asked him to apply for a role as a corporate lawyer he jumped at the opportunity as a way of saving face. Three years on, having made a successful transition, he was asked to take on a general management role within the business. His former legal colleagues were appalled at what they saw as a loss in his professional status. His coach, seeing him struggle with the idea of letting go of his identity as a lawyer, asked him, 'What will becoming a General Manager get you?'. He answered:

- An escape from seeing myself as a failing lawyer.
- A challenge that could never have been available to me if I had stayed with the City law firm.
- A bigger salary and bonus than I ever imagined.
- International assignments.

It was important for Hugh to recognize what taking a difficult decision would get him, as it bolstered him when meeting with legal colleagues, who had an investment in wanting to see him as a failed Partner, rather than someone who had moved on. Looking at what letting go of his legal identity got him, motivated him to succeed in his new responsibilities rather than seeing it as the second best option.

EXERCISE

Ask a friend to identify something in their life they would like to set a goal for. You may want to suggest examples, e.g. keeping in touch with friends more often, writing a book, going away on holiday alone, learning a musical instrument. Then ask them the question:

What will achieving that goal mean for you?

Encourage them to offer more than one answer.

When they have exhausted their responses, ask them the alternate question:

What will getting the goal get you?

Listen to how different their responses are to the first and second questions.

Ask them which response is the most motivating in terms of them committing to action.

Their response will depend on their own model of motivation. There is no better or worse question.

As a coach you are looking for the question that is most meaningful for the particular individual in unleashing their commitment to act on their solution. It is important to address motivation as part of solution building. Motivation drives commitment to the solution, and ensures that the scale of the solution matches with the size of motivation.

Summary

Solutions emerge naturally from the work that the coach has done in Stages I and II of the coaching process. Solution building is led by the coachee drawing on the resources that the Manager Coach has made them aware of through skilled questioning and listening.

The process of solution building is facilitated through:

- Using scaling as a means of defining the degree of change that the individual is motivated to achieve, and looking at the solutions they can apply to making the shift.
- The Miracle Question allows the individual to create a future in which the change has happened, as a means of identifying what they want to do differently.
- Re-using skills introduced in Stage II – in particular the use of exception seeking to find resources to apply to achieving the target.
- Helping the individual find the commitment to act through asking them to define what achieving the goal will get them and will mean to them.

References

1. Berg, L.K. (1994) *Family Based Services: A Solutions Focused Approach.* Norton.
2. Jackson, P.Z. and McKergow, M. (2002) *The Solutions Focus: The Simple Way to Positive Change.* Nicholas Brearley.
3. de Shazer, S. (1988) *Clues: Investigating Solutions in Brief Therapy.* Norton.
4. Armstrong, L. (2001) *It's Not About the Bike: My Journey Back to Life.* Yellow Jersey Press.

11

Delivery

Failure should be our teacher, not our undertaker. Failure is delay not defeat.
It is a temporary detour, not a dead end. Failure is something we can avoid
only by saying nothing, doing nothing, and being nothing.

Denis Waitley

Effective coaching leads to action. Insight and learning without action is failure both for the coach and the coachee. The STARTED process asks you to hold back from the instinct to move into action until you are clear that the individual has identified their real target, and identified solutions of a kind and size that motivate their desire to act. It would seem that the work is now done, other than to offer words of encouragement. Wrong. Delivery requires as much of the coach as the other stages. In particular, the final stage asks you to stay involved and to continue to coach when action does not get the results intended.

It is common to see the action focused stage as involving little more than the invocation of SMART, through asking the coachee to identify:

- What specifically they are going to do?
- How much of it?
- By when?

The agreement is committed to paper, and the task of the individual is to report back on progress. The assumption being that planning ensures success. It is a belief with a long pedigree: from Benjamin Franklin's, 'By failing to prepare, you are preparing to fail', to a Barclays Bank advertising hoarding stating, 'A goal without a plan is just a dream'.

Planning based on identified actions is a necessity of the transfer from insight to action, but it is not sufficient. It is insufficient because it ignores the reality of change, and particularly of behavioural change. It is difficult to do, and even harder to sustain. As a Manager Coach it is sustained change you are seeking. Desired behaviour that happens only when you are available to provide support is a recipe for high-maintenance coaching and employee dependency. You can afford neither. In order to build self-sustenance, your task as a coach at this final stage is to focus less on the plan and more on what could cause the plan to fail.

This may seem unnecessary. After all your hard work, this should be the stage when the work passes back to the coachee for them to show that they can deliver the solution, which you have helped them identify; the point at which you can turn back to all the other demands on your time. However, if your time is to have been well spent you need to stay engaged a little longer, to help deal with the reality of doing things differently.

A focus solely on agreeing a task list ignores that which was known as far back as the 4th century BC when Aristotle wrote, 'It is easy to perform a good action, but not easy to acquire a settled habit of performing such actions'. Any reader who has been involved in a change programme knows that such programmes are expensive exercises with variable results, as the clear logic of the planning process collides with the wondrous complexity of human behaviour. It is why quick-fix approaches do not work. Employees are not persuaded to give up well-embedded beliefs and ways of doing things, even if they recognize the business imperative, through management messages in company newsletters, half-day seminars or inspirational t-shirts. Change requires sustained effort with constant reinforcement and flexing of approach in response to the feedback. It is less a relentless drive in getting from A to B than a process of navigation, changing tack in response to the prevailing conditions, so that the route to B adjusts in response to learning from success and failure.

Similarly, the staff member now has a clear sense of what they want to achieve and how they think they can do it, but it has yet to be tested out. When it is tested it starts to unsettle. It unsettles the individual because it is unfamiliar and challenging, and it unsettles those around them because it is unexpected. Machiavelli wrote,

> There is nothing more difficult to handle, more doubtful of success, nor more dangerous to carry through than initiating changes ... The innovator makes enemies of all those who prospered under the old order, and only lukewarm support is forthcoming from those who would prosper under the new.[1]

Machiavelli's assessment is as true of the individual who struggles within themselves on the value of changing (as did Hugh in Chapter 10), as it is of institutions seeking to change. For all that the individual expresses a strong desire to change, unless the reality of human behaviour within change is addressed, the Manager Coach risks the warm feelings that a good coaching conversation engenders petering away when action does not follow words.

Understanding what happens when individuals attempt to change is important. The evidence on those who attempt to give up smoking is that, on average, there will be five failed attempts before they finally succeed.[2] The evidence on sustained weight loss is even more damning: 95 per cent of slimmers regain the weight they lose.[3] This is despite every one of those individuals being determined on day one that this time things will be different. The explanation for this collapse between intent and delivery is explained in a model of behaviour change that identifies six stages:[4]

1. *Pre-contemplation.* Here the individual is engaged in a behaviour they wish to change, e.g. 'I wish I was less impatient with staff who waste my time'. Implicit in the 'wish' is any lack of intent to change behaviour.

2. *Contemplation.* At this stage the individual starts to consider the possibility of changing. They may state their intention to change. 'I am going to try and be less snappy with people.' However, they also see the advantages of staying as they are. 'Being snappy keeps people out of my way and gets me time.'

3. *Preparation.* Here the individual takes some steps to change their behaviour. They make minor adjustments to their thought patterns, e.g. they may come up with a plan for change, but they have yet to seriously adjust their behaviour. Often individuals who ask for coaching are at this stage. They report, 'I have tried hard in the last couple of weeks not to snap off the heads of team members whose work is less than I would expect, but it is difficult'. That is why asking individuals what they have already done to address the problem they bring is a useful means of testing out if they are already in preparation, or at an earlier stage of behaviour change.

4. *Action.* Here the individual is actively engaged in the new behaviour. They have found their target and identified ways of meeting it. They may also be looking to find ways of overcoming the problems that would stop them maintaining the new behaviour. The snappy colleague reports that they schedule time with staff for times of the day when they know their blood sugar won't be low, as their irritability increases with hunger.

However, the research evidence is that Action is the least stable stage and is associated with the highest risk of relapse.[5] The snappy colleague finds that the effort of being conscious of their actions becomes too much at times, and that there is something comfortably familiar in lashing out at a direct report when they underperform. Alternately, they find that when they try out the new behaviour it does not get the response they expect, so there is no immediate reinforcement to their acting differently.

5. *Maintenance.* This is the stage at which an individual sustains behavioural change over time. The individual works to prevent relapse and to reinforce the gains of the Action stage. The snappy colleague reports that staff have mentioned that they seem different and more relaxed. They report that when they feel themselves wanting to lacerate with their tongue, they focus on what they want to achieve longer term, rather than the immediate relief that lashing out gives them.

6. *Termination.* Here there is a perceived absence of the temptation to behave in the old way. The head biter reports that they can't remember the last time they wanted to wound with words a staff member who had failed to deliver, because they now have a better repertoire of choices for getting staff to raise their performance.

The coaching process so far has taken the individual to the point of action. It is important that the Manager Coach is not now cajoled into a false sense of security, since with this will come feelings of annoyance when action is not delivered smoothly. Recognizing that Action is an exciting stage for the individual in terms of their motivation, but also a stage where some failure is an inevitable part of the process, allows the coach to build-in additional frameworks that they can use in helping the individual move towards Maintenance and Termination.

Managing action

The rest of this chapter is concerned with the inputs the coach can make that reduce the likelihood of failure, and of ways of dealing with it positively when it does occur, so that the coachee does not become derailed from their intent.

Minimizing the possibility of failure begins within the action planning stage. The emergence of solutions leads naturally to identifying the tasks that need to be done in delivering the solution. The nature of the solution will also define timeframes. For the coach, the tasks and the timeline for achieving them may seem self-evident. It is important, however, that the task list is created by the coachee and that they recognize that in creating it they will be held to account for it.

The quantum question:

What are you going to be accountable for?

focuses the coachee on creating a list that they take ownership of, knowing that they will be held to account. It acts as a brake on setting tasks that are beyond their own sense of realism and achievability.

Sample Dialogue

Through the coaching conversation, the coachee has defined that their best way forward is to look for an opportunity within the parent company that will involve them in working outside the UK.

The coach asks them to define what they now need to do.

Coachee: I need to put in a call to the corporate HQ to get a sense of what is happening in New York. I could do that this week.

Coach: Who do you know in corporate HQ?

Coachee: No-one, but I did once see the CEO when he gave a presentation here. I could call his office and ask for some leads.

Coach: What else would help you?

Coachee: I need to put together my c.v., but it needs to be different from the one I have done in the past because that just lists jobs. I need something which focuses on the skills I am wanting to make more use of, and shows how I have applied them in the past.

Coach: Yes, a performance focused c.v. would be of more value to you. When could you do that?

Coachee: This weekend.

Coach: What else?

Coachee: I want to talk with someone who has gone from the UK out to New York to get an insider track on what it is like making that kind of move, and how they have made it work.

Coach: Who could help you do that?

Coachee: I can ask HR to put me in touch with someone.

> *Coach:* So you have talked about calling the CEO's office, revising your c.v. this weekend, and getting a contact from HR. What do you want to be accountable for when we touch base next week?
>
> *Coachee:* Put like that, it looks a bit different. I don't know if I would feel comfortable calling the CEO's office. His PA would probably just swat me away, and I don't expect he would respond to an email from someone he does not know. Perhaps it is more realistic to try and find someone in my department, like that woman who worked in New York a couple of years ago. I could ask her what she knows about what is happening, and whether she could put me in touch with someone there who I could chat to. I could do that by next week.
>
> *Coach:* And your c.v.?
>
> *Coachee:* I have no idea how to present my experience differently. I think I should look on the internet to get an idea of formats, and then do a draft. I could do that and show it to you by next week.
>
> *Coach:* Talking with HR?
>
> *Coachee:* Well, it would probably be a better conversation if I had a different sort of c.v. and gave them a sense of what I am looking for, rather than just asking for a meeting and hoping they can work out who would be the best person for me to talk with. So I don't want to be accountable for talking with HR by next week.
>
> *Coach:* Is that enough?
>
> *Coachee:* Yes, that's clearer, and I am more likely to do it.

Alternately, the accountability question can be used to raise the bar on actions. In asking the question, the individual reconsiders the tasks they have set themselves, and recognizes that they have set tasks with insufficient stretch and that they have the resources to take on more.

This is different from the coach pushing the staff member to do more, even if you know they are capable of more. The danger for the coach is that if the coach becomes involved in defining the task list, they also become emotionally attached to it and any failure to deliver will have an impact on the coaching relationship because they will have failed you. A task list that is generated by the staff member is their list. You will have no emotional attachment to it other than whether it enables them to achieve their target. If they fail to deliver on their tasks, you will be able to take a detached position in helping them find a way forward. If they have failed to deliver on your task you are working from a second position. If you have ever counselled a friend who is unhappy with their work, you will know that the hours invested in listening to them telling you how awful their boss is, and your sound advice to quit and move on, leads to feelings of frustration when the friend consistently fails to act on your insight. Conversely, when they do eventually leave their job, they will give little recognition for your input six months previously. You were asking them to take Action, at a point when they were still Pre-contemplating.

Coaches can offer suggestions for action if the individual clearly shows that they are at the Action stage but are stuck as to how they can make solutions actionable. The key lies in being willing to make an offer without an investment in the offer being accepted. The coach has to be open to the rejection. So that, following rejection, the coach can then ask,

What do you want to do instead?

It is a question to be offered, not in a tone of exasperation, but in a way that suggests your offer will have helped them clarify what they now need to do.

Return to scaling

The Manager Coach has helped the individual to move to a point where they are able to define a task list that has a good likelihood of success, because it is their list and they are happy to be accountable for it. There is one further check on the likelihood of action, through the application of scaling. Having stated what they are going to do, the coachee is feeling confident of success. Back on the job, those accountabilities can start to feel different. What looked low risk within a safe coaching conversation can feel very different once the individual is acting alone. For this reason, scaling is valuable as a means of establishing confidence to act in the ways they have outlined, following the pattern of:

- establishing the scale
- establishing where they are against that scale

- establishing where they need to be to act
- discovering what will make the difference in moving up the scale.

CASE STUDY

Keiko was a Japanese entrant to the highly competitive management programme of an investment bank. She had a first-class economics degree from a British university and was extremely conscientious. She was recognized by her peers as very able, but each time there was a new placement within the programme, she found that less able but more outspoken peers were getting the placements she would have liked. She held back, wanting to be invited in, where others went and knocked on the door demanding entry. Through a coaching session she came to realize that she had to be able to talk about what she had contributed rather than hoping others would do that for her. She outlined a list of tasks she could do that would increase the likelihood of getting a higher-profile placement. She seemed happy with them and was about to leave when her coach asked, 'Once you get back to your desk, how confident are you on a scale of 0 to 10 that you will act on what we have agreed?'. At this point Keiko's face dropped. She looked embarrassed. 'If I am honest, I would say it is 4.'

Invited to tell the coach what 4 represented, she started by outlining all her personal limitations as an introvert, who found it difficult to talk about herself. Encouraged to look at the resources that contributed to her being at 4 rather than 2 or 1, she recognized that she had a good reputation with the organizer of the graduate scheme, and that she had done some work that she could talk about comfortably. Asked to define where she needed to be in order to do those things she had put on her task list, she identified 8 as her desired point. Invited to state what would increase her confidence so that she could be an 8, she spoke of listing all the things she had enjoyed being part of, so that she could show enthusiasm when she spoke; writing down what development she wanted from her next assignment so that she did not have to think on the spot; telling herself she had the same right to a good placement as everyone else in her group; and reminding herself that her performance reports had been outstanding, so she was not trying to trick anyone into giving her anything she did not deserve.

By being allowed to admit the gap between intention and confidence, Keiko was able to find ways of bolstering confidence so that she got the placement she wanted. Without the scaling, she risked reverting to her old patterns of behaviour once away from the protection of the coaching conversation.

Scaffolding

Encouraging individuals to address the gap between intention and action allows for finding ways to provide scaffolding that will support action. Scaffolding means inviting the coachee to identify things that will give them the focus and discipline to act. We all use scaffolding every day. By setting the alarm clock we ensure getting up in time to get to work. By defining the length of time we are willing to give to a piece of work we structure our attention on delivery. By setting up time-management systems we define which work we do first. Asking a coachee to think of ways that will provide the scaffolding that will help them commit to act, produces wonderfully idiosyncratic responses:

- Writing up the actions on post-its stuck to my PC so I can't avoid them.
- Telling my colleagues so they will know if I don't do as I say.
- Writing affirmations to encourage myself.
- Wearing my lucky shoes/suit/tie/earrings when I know I have to do the difficult things.
- Buying some expensive chocolate and putting it on my desk, but not allowing myself to eat it until I do what I say I am going to do.

Writing this book, a task I had committed to several years ago with little evidence of action, began to happen when I scaffolded. I put a timetable on the office wall with deadlines for each chapter, a weekly word target and space for recording how many words I had written. Suddenly the paralysis gap between desire to write and confidence to do so disappeared, as the motivation to fill in that word chart each week structured action.

All of the coach's actions so far have been focused on minimizing the likelihood of failure to act, through creating a number of opportunities for the coachee to check themselves, by resizing their actions, scaling their confidence and creating scaffolding that supports action. This increases the likelihood that success will follow. Where the intended target is a long-established behaviour change, a painless transition is unlikely and relapses highly probable. The Manager Coach's role is then to keep the coachee focused on success and the learning from failure.

Learning from failure

Lines such as 'There is no failure only feedback', sound glib, but beneath the strapline lies truth. Simon Woodruffe, founder of the Japanese restaurant chain 'Yo Sushi' says, 'I have met all sorts of people in business. The thing I have learnt is that successful people don't go around succeeding all day. Successful people fail'.[6] They fail because they risk, and they use failure as a means of providing learning, rather than seeing it as an assessment of their capability. For further evidence look no further than J.F. Kennedy, defeated in the election for class president at his college; J.K. Rowling, whose first Harry Potter novel was rejected by numerous publishers; or Elvis Presley, who was told by his teacher that he could not sing. Successful people fail because they invest themselves in taking repeated action, despite failure, in order to achieve something that is important to them.

Coaching encourages the other person to risk doing something differently in order to achieve a reward that has meaning for them. In taking that risk, they may fail at the first attempts, or succeed and then relapse. It is here that the Manager Coach has a key role in supporting successful delivery through applying their skills to keep the other person focused on success.

Failing at the first attempt

Having invested time and effort in helping a staff member to understand what they need to do, it is disheartening when they report back that they have not done what they set out to do. It is easy to quickly move from being the non-judgemental enabler to the highly judgemental critic. This response highlights that you have become invested in their success, even if only because it will reduce the time you have to give them. Operating from a judgemental position will not help them. When they fail to deliver, your task is to suspend judgement and to help their understanding of what has got in the way of success, so that they can remove that barrier.

The six-stage plan of change management highlights that the Action stage is unstable. It is unstable because no matter how high the motivation, there is always a competing commitment – to stay doing what they have always done. When a staff member touches base to report back on progress, if they have failed to take action they will explain it away:

- I would have but . . .
- I tried to make the time but . . .
- I thought about doing it but . . .
- It just wasn't possible.
- An opportunity did not arise.
- They made it impossible for me to . . .

What they are saying, although they will not recognize this, is that they have a stronger commitment to an alternative. In order to move the coachee beyond this roadblock, it is important to help them understand the nature of this block, and how they can break it up.

The process starts from challenging their thoughts, through openly addressing their competing commitment.

SAMPLE DIALOGUE

Dorothy has had 360-degree feedback that she does not listen to her staff, and that this impacts on their motivation. It is also reflected in higher than average staff turnover numbers. Through coaching she comes to recognize that there is value in showing to staff that she does listen to them, and she commits to setting up a number of one-to-one meetings with her staff to get an understanding of the problems they are facing with customers. When she meets her coach again, it becomes clear that she has not held any meetings. This is explained away by her work schedule.

Coach: Dorothy, what are you committed to?

Dorothy: I am committed to being a good leader, and I know that means I should listen more.

Coach: Should listen more?

Dorothy: No, I mean I can see the value in listening if it helps me solve some of the problems we face.

Coach: That is why we agreed you would institute some one-to-ones and you have not made time to do any, so what stopped you doing that?

Dorothy: It's just time. I have been too busy.

Coach: I don't buy that. You make time for what is important to you. What stopped you setting up those meetings?

Dorothy: I don't know, I just wasn't sure they would tell me more than I already know.

Coach: That's a possibility. I am interested in what was a more compelling commitment, because if you were not spending time with staff you were choosing to do other things.

Dorothy: I am always committed to delivery, and I will do whatever it takes to hit those numbers.

Coach: What is the pull of that commitment – of delivering on the task?

Dorothy: I believe that delivering on the task is what will get me a promotion. I suppose I think that listening to staff could deflect me from what I am wanting to achieve. I think I also believe that delivery on task is easier than dealing with people.

Once the competing commitment is found, the reason for its power becomes transparent. For as long as Dorothy believes that staff risk deflecting her from the task delivery from which her career progression will come, and that people are less controllable than task outcomes, her reasons for not setting up one-to-one meetings become entirely logical.

Having unearthed the competing commitment, the Manager Coach can now hold that commitment up for closer examination.

Coach: So there are some good reasons that explain why you did not hold those meetings. Thank you for explaining them to me. Which of those was the biggest barrier to your setting up those meetings?

Dorothy: The belief that it is delivering on task which gets promotion, at the end of the day.

Coach: Just look at that belief for a minute. Is it true that delivery on task is the only thing that affects promotion?

Dorothy: Well maybe in the past it was, but especially now we have 360-degree appraisal and a new competency framework, I am not sure it is so true. There are good task people who have not got promotions recently because they are seen as poor people managers.

Coach: So delivery on the task is not enough?

Dorothy: Maybe not – which takes me back to my commitment to being a good leader.

Coach: So I am wondering what would help you commit to being a good leader?

Dorothy: That's hard. I think it is accepting that while people are difficult to manage, I can achieve more for my own career with them than without them.

Coach: So if you know that people are difficult but that you can achieve more with them than without them, what can you commit to do?

Dorothy: OK, I get it. It makes sense to have those meetings, but I think I need some help in how to structure them so they have an outcome and I don't think I am wasting time. I also need help in how to manage myself so that I stay listening.

Helping the coachee to state the competing commitment, rather than allowing them to explain away failure, is a powerful way of moving the person back on track against their target. Once the competing commitment is unearthed, the reason for failure to deliver becomes obvious. What else would they do? In the same way as Jacqueline was only able to properly address her reluctance to commit to an MBA once she was allowed to honestly address her assumption of the inevitable spinsterhood of successful women (Chapter 6), coachees are able to remove the obstacle of the competing commitment, once they are given permission to state it.

Working with partial success

The hope of every coachee is that the outcome of the conversation will be the implementation of the action plan, with the desired consequences. Sometimes this happens. More often there is, at the first attempt, partial success. The plan they have created in their head, the conversation they had practised internally, the time and the place they had imagined for the encounter, do not happen according to plan. They find themselves caught off-guard by the timing, or the response they get is not what they had hoped for. In reporting back, they confuse a failed attempt with personal failure. The challenge for the Manager Coach now is to help them find the learning that has come from failure, so that they see it as a temporary state rather than a dead end. The Manager Coach also looks to challenge their assessment of the attempt, by asking them to take a reality bite view of their effort to do something different.

Complimenting

Given that a principle of solution focused coaching is the focus on the coachee's resources, it is important to highlight to coachees the resources they have used, regardless of the success of the attempt. This is not flattery; it is a way of helping the coachee break out of the black and white focus set up by their internal critic. Neither is complimenting motivated by a desire to be kind, or to rescue the staff member from their feelings of failure. Complimenting is a reality-based process. It is based on what the coachee tells you about the risk they took in committing to action.[7]

SAMPLE DIALOGUE

Moira had struggled in her role as a female Senior Director working within a very male culture. She saw herself as on the edge and discounted by her male colleagues, and particularly the CEO. Her reaction was to become angry and then to cry. This would be followed by weeks of self-doubt when she would make herself ill with anxiety. She compensated by driving herself hard in order to prove that she deserved to be in her role. The action she had committed to was to express her views at a Board meeting, holding her emotions in check by trying to stand outside herself. This was a wholly new way of behaving in that situation and, when she reports back, her demeanour as she comes into the room signals failure.

Coach: You set yourself a big challenge when we last met. I am wondering how it went?

Moira: Complete disaster.

Coach: Complete disaster?

Moira: Yes. They did not agree with me and I got angry.

Coach: Well first of all. What I am hearing is that you took the risk of trying to behave differently in a situation that is very difficult for you (*compliment*).

Moira: Well that's true, but I could not do everything we talked about, so I came out feeling a failure.

Coach: You did not do everything we talked about, but tell me what you did do?

Moira: I made sure that I got into the discussion early on, and I couched my contributions in corporate terms, rather than just thinking about what it meant for my area.

Coach: You had clearly thought through how you were going to intervene (*compliment*).

Moira: Yes, I had spent time before the meeting thinking about the agenda, and I had thought about the things that engage them, and the things I do that turn them off.

Coach: So you had a clear plan of how you were going to behave, based on looking at things from their perspective (*compliment*).

Moira: So that's why I feel mad with myself, for losing the plot when their responses were anything but corporate. Once they started rejecting my thoughts from their own silo perspective, I thought what is the point, and I reverted back to my usual style.

Coach: How long do you think you held out for?

Moira: I would say about 30 minutes.

Coach: So for 30 minutes you were able to hold on to behaving differently when they made no attempts to change. That must have been hard work (*compliment*).

Moira: It was – but in a strange way, I enjoyed being able to stand outside it all, and watch myself behaving differently. If only they had been willing to give something back, I would have held on longer.

Coach: So standing outside yourself does seem to help you hold onto trying new things. What did you notice about yourself when you were standing outside?

Moira: Thinking about it now, I noticed that I was very calm and engaged. Those first 30 minutes were fun, because I looked at it as an experiment with me as the detached scientist. It was only when I forgot I was in an experiment, and got involved emotionally that it stopped being fun.

Coach: Looking at it as an experiment sounds like a good way of not investing yourself in the outcome (*compliment*). What have your learnt from this experiment that will be helpful to your next one?

Moira: I have learnt that I should probably not have started with the whole group, I should experiment on a one-to-one basis first. I have learnt that even with this group, I can behave differently if I view myself as a detached observer. I have learnt I can be responsive and corporate for 30 minutes, even when they are not. So next time, I will aim for 45 minutes, and see if I hold out longer, whether or not they start to change their reactions. I also learnt, strangely, that when I was focused on the

> experiment I was less aware of me as a woman and them as men, because I was more interested in their behaviour. Maybe, I was better than I thought.
>
> *Coach:* Is that a surprise to you?
>
> *Moira:* Not now that I can see the picture differently.
>
> *Coach:* So what you are telling me now is this was not a failure. You know, Thomas Edison, the inventor, when challenged on his success rate, is reported to have said that 'He had not failed, he had found 10 000 ways that did not work', and it was from those failures that success eventually came.

There are two types of compliment a coach can use. The *direct* compliment is a positive reaction to what is being told by the staff member. An example of this is the coach's comment to Moira that 'Looking at it as an experiment seems like a good way of not investing yourself in the outcome', or 'You took the risk of trying to behave differently'. These type of compliments work when:

- they spring directly from what the coachee has said
- they reflect what the coachee values.

There is no value in showering compliments in the scatter-gun hope that more is better. It is the quality and authenticity of the compliments that is important. One compliment that directly links with what is important to the coachee is more powerful than ten automatic 'Wows' or 'Greats'.

The second type of compliment is an *indirect* compliment. An indirect compliment is a question that implies something positive about the coachee. The Coach's invitation to Moira, 'What did you notice about yourself when you were standing outside?' is an indirect compliment: it suggests that she is bound to have noticed something different by taking up a new position. Indirect compliments are more powerful than direct compliments, because in asking the question the coachee is able to discover and claim their own resources. It is when Moira sees the strength in being a scientist rather than a player, that she is able to start defining the learning that has come out of the experiment.

There is a third sort of compliment. Coachees may use a *self-compliment*. When Moira reported that 'Maybe, I was better than I thought', she was self-complimenting. Self-compliments are valuable to a coach because they signal signs of progress. The coach can then follow up with an indirect compliment, such as 'Is that a surprise to you?', as a way of encouraging reinforcement of the strengths that Moira is beginning to see.

The challenge for the Manager Coach

Offering compliments is not a highly developed habit in British culture. There is a fear that it signals sycophancy and insincerity. There is an added dimension when the compliment is given across genders. Will the intent be misunderstood? The focus on pointing out what is wrong, rather than pointing the light at what is working, is a much more strongly developed muscle in UK organizational thinking. The challenge for the Manager Coach is to use compliments consciously as part of the process of learning from failure.

The solution focused approach does not use compliments because they make the coachee like the coach or to take away the pain of failure. Compliments are a means of helping the coachee to notice change when they cannot see it; to recognize resources when they overlook them; and to see strength where they only look for weakness.

Given that the coachee may well be unused to compliments, their first response can be to dismiss them as not important, 'It was nothing/I hardly did anything/I did not do it very well'. The coachee does not have to accept the compliment, but they will hear it, provided that the compliment is based in the reality of what the coachee has presented to the coach. It is the difference between:

> *Coach I:* Well first of all. What I am hearing is that you took the risk of trying to behave differently in a situation, which is very difficult for you.

Compliment based on direct reportage of the coachee

and

> *Coach II:* I bet you did a whole lot better than you imagined, and you did not really fail at all.

Compliment that ignores the coachee's reality.

Listen for examples of failure being reported to you by a staff member. Rather than looking to minimize the failure in order to make them feel better, ask them to describe what they did and then:

- Offer a direct compliment based on the reality they have described to you.
- Offer an indirect compliment through asking a question that invites them to identify the resources they brought to their attempt.
- Notice how the staff member reacts to your compliments.
- Notice your own comfort/discomfort.
- What can you compliment yourself on in how you carried out the exercise?

Success and then relapse

Knowing that the Action stage almost inevitably involves relapse, the Manager Coach works with that reality in order to get the coachee back on track as quickly as possible. Sports trainers know that every sportsperson, no matter how committed, will have times when they break out of the schedule; when the discipline gets too much, the diet too restrictive and the restrictions on their social life too limiting. Because they know this they accept the breakout, and focus instead on how quickly they can get them back on course, so that they do not lose the habit of a disciplined life or sight of their goals. Similarly, if the Manager Coach accepts that relapse is part of the story of moving into new ways of behaving, they can build it into the delivery stage. Relapse does not mean failure. It means there are times when it is easier to do what is comfortable, even if dysfunctional, rather than what is harder work in the short term, for a longer-term payoff.

A way of helping the coachee to move beyond the relapse is to give them responsibility for coaching themselves back on course.

SAMPLE DIALOGUE

Julian had worked hard to engage in the people-management aspects of his role. As a technical specialist who thrived on crises, he had little interest in the day-to-day realities of managing people, but he had come to see that when he ignored those aspects his staff became demotivated, turnover increased and performance dropped. His target was for his department to show up as above average in the organization's staff satisfaction survey. His actions towards achieving that had focused on making time for regular performance review sessions with staff, and dealing with people issues when they arose rather than hoping they would go away.

He had made progress, and had even reported some enjoyment of getting to know his staff better. At the next coaching session, he reported that he could see himself reverting back to his old ways because they were less time-demanding.

Coach: Tell me what you have reverted back to?

Julian: The last few weeks there has been a big crisis on because market conditions are worsening. I have been pulled into working on our response, and I have really enjoyed feeling I am at the heart of things and that my expertise counts. It's meant I have been out of the department a lot, and I know things have been happening while I have been away. I pick up the signs, but I am ignoring them because it will deflect me from what I have to do.

Coach: I notice that you recognize that your absence makes a difference, and that while you have done nothing, you are picking up on what's happening. You would not have said those things six months ago.

Julian: You're right, six months ago I would just have been pleased to have something to do that did not involve managing people.

Coach: So what are you committed to now Julian?

Julian: I am still committed to having a department that is well managed, and that shows up well in the staff satisfaction results.

Coach: What about your competing commitment to the crisis?

Julian: It's exciting, but I know it's short term. I will always be drawn towards those things, but I am clear that performance relies on my committing to managing.

Coach: Does saying that surprise you?

Julian: It does and it doesn't. I guess it shows that I have made some progress in the last six months.

Coach: Because you have made progress, I think you can solve this present difficulty. I would like you to imagine that you are watching a video of yourself in the department over the last few weeks. As your own coach what do you notice, and what feedback can you give?

Julian: This feels a bit odd, but I will try. I notice I am not there very often, and when I am there I hurry to my PC and am head down the whole time. I notice that no-one is talking to me, and that there is lots of stuff going on around that I have no idea about. I notice that most of the time my being there does not make people come and make demands on me – in fact the reverse. They seem to be mainly getting on fine. In fact the more I look, the more I realize that the person who is most missing out is me.

Coach: That is an interesting observation that in becoming more detached from the department, your staff are doing fine without you, but you may be missing out. As your own coach, what feedback can you now give Julian?

Julian: I want to tell him that he needs to let his staff know what he is doing – or as much as is appropriate – and to tell them when this diversion will end. Strangely, I also want to tell him to let his staff know that he misses knowing what is going on, and would like them to keep him informed. I want to tell him that he needs to show that he is still engaged in managing them, and that means he wants to know when things are not working. I also want to tell him to start the performance review discussions again, maybe not next week, but he should make it clear to staff that this is a temporary blip, and does not represent how things are going to be in the future. How does that sound?

Coach: It sounds very clear. What do you need to do now?

Julian: I need to turn this into some concrete actions that I can build into the next few days.

In this conversation, the coach drew on techniques we have previously used. They complimented Julian on his progress and they checked out his commitment to managing and the power of the competing commitment. The additional tool brought to the coaching conversation was to introduce the idea of self-coaching. Because Julian now has experience of taking action towards his intended target, he has experiences he can call on to coach himself back on track. By using the idea of watching himself on video, the coach is asking Julian to take a detached observer position. From this position, he is able to describe rather than judge, and in the process of observation he identifies what he needs to do differently.

EXERCISE

Think of a situation where you have taken action towards effecting a change in your behaviour, and where progress is not smooth. Along with movement towards the intended target, there are also times of relapse. Identify a specific example, and project it onto a video screen in front of you.

- What do you notice that person doing when they relapse?
- What constructive feedback can you give them to help them back on track?

Maintenance

Getting beyond the instability of the Action phase to the self-regulation of the Maintenance phase as quickly as possible is important for the Manager Coach. Maintenance comes when the individual has received sufficient rewards from behaving differently, of the kinds they value, that they come to believe the effort is worthwhile. Maintenance is helped by an awareness of the resources they use to act in the desired way, and to overcome the inevitable times of difficulty. Supporting that move demands that the coach periodically ask the coachee to identify:

- What is doing things differently getting you/meaning for you? (*reward identification*)
- What are you doing that enables you to . . .? (*resource seeking*)
- How do you resist the urge to do things the old way? (*relapse resources*)

- What do you do to get yourself back on track when things don't work out? (*scaffolding*)

CASE STUDY

Charley had asked his manager to coach him after a department away-day where he was confronted about his attitude towards his colleagues. Outside of work he was charming, but when he was put together with a group of peers, his inner piranha appeared. He blocked out any emotional intelligence in his desire to prove he could do more, faster and better than anyone else. When confronted by his peers, Charley was at first highly defensive, explaining away his behaviours by their inadequacies, before finally accepting that if everyone saw him this way he clearly had a problem. He left the meeting severely bruised. It took a couple of conversations before Charley recognized that his target was to bring the interpersonal skills he used outside of work into his work. He identified situations in which this could be helpful, and he established a hierarchy of which colleagues it would be more or less difficult to do this with. Starting with the easiest, he used what he learnt from each encounter to take on more demanding situations. When he had a disastrous meeting with a colleague from another department who he saw as lacking any clarity about what they were trying to achieve, he self-coached to realize that the individual was in an impossible job with constantly changing objectives. Looked at this way, their lack of clarity was understandable. He invited them to lunch, acknowledged that he had made the last meeting difficult, and asked if he could help in some way. That invitation allowed Charley to offer his colleague coaching on how to deal with their work situation. Over time, Charley came to recognize the resources he used to work well with people, and was able to apply them to a much wider range of situations than his original target. He also came to enjoy the feelings he got from understanding others, and using that understanding, to help get his job done. When his manager asked him a year on what he remembered of their coaching conversations, Charley remembered very little of what had happened, other than that he was asked really good questions. So effective had been the manager's coaching that the process had been invisible to him. What he did recognize was that the person he had now become at work was very different from the person of a year ago, and that that person was more effective.

Summary

Delivery in coaching often focuses on the logistics of action planning, but this is insufficient because it fails to address the real difficulties of changing behaviour and sustaining that change. Drawing on what has been learnt from studies of effecting sustained behavioural change, the chapter offered techniques for:

- Scoping accountability through differentiating between actions that could be taken, and actions that the individual is willing to be accountable for.
- Scaling confidence to act, so that the supports to confidence can be found.
- Scaffolding actions to sustain motivation.
- Addressing failure through making visible the power of the competing commitment.
- Using partial success as a basis for learning through the focused application of compliments.
- Using relapses as a source of self-coaching.

References

1. Machiavelli, N. (2003) *The Prince.* Penguin Classics, p. 21.
2. Constantine, L.M. and Scott, S. (1992) *When Survivors Quit Smoking.* Moving Forward. 2(4). Available at http://movingforward.org/v2n4-health. html.
3. Cummins, L. (2003) *The Diet Business: Banking on Failure.* BBC Online Business News, 5 February.
4. Prochaska, J.O. and Clemente, C.C. (1997) The transtheoretical model of behavior change. *American Journal of Health,* 12, 38–48.
5. Prochascka, J.O. and Clemente, C.C. (1985) Common processes of self change in smoking, weight control and psychological distress. In Shiffman, S. and Willis, T.A. (eds) *Coping and Substance Abuse.* Academic Press, pp. 345–63.
6. Simon Woodruffe, speaking at the Institute of Directors Annual Conference, London, April 2005.
7. de Jong, P. and Berg, I.K. (2002) *Interviewing for Solutions.* Brooks Cole.

12

Leadership and coaching

Leadership is lifting a person's vision to higher sights, the raising of a person's performance to a higher standard, the building of a personality beyond it's normal limitations.

Peter F. Drucker

The process of STARTED is now complete. The reader who has followed the structure and is now willing to try out coaching tools in their conversations with staff is no different from their own staff in their likely response to acquiring new behaviours. They may have started reading this book from the position of, 'I know managers are expected to coach staff' (pre-contemplation). They may have recognized their own resistance to the process: 'I know coaching is seen as a good thing these days, but it just encourages staff to moan instead of getting on with things' (contemplation). They may have come to the book at a point where they have thought about trying out some new things in discussions with staff, but have not followed it through (preparation). Success means being motivated to take action, but the evidence tells us that the Action stage is likely to be one of partial success and occasional failure. Sustaining yourself through this stage to the point where the behaviours are self-maintaining requires support. This comes from there being valued rewards for moving beyond the familiar and comfortable. The most powerful of rewards is a sense that there is some personal benefit in doing things differently.

So far the focus has been on the role of coaching in capturing the motivation of the talented, and working with the expectations of the post-baby-boomer workers. This risks presenting coaching as a 'hygiene' or 'maintenance factor',[1] i.e. something managers now have to do as a means of getting work done; another skill in their competence set, alongside prioritization and time management. As a motivator for the individual manager, this is likely to be limited in its appeal. A more powerful motivator is the link between coaching and leadership, since there is powerful evidence that coaching is a key element of effective leadership. Managers who aspire to be seen as leaders are helped by the application of coaching skills.

Asking managers to describe the best manager they have ever experienced rarely elicits warm stories of the manager who never went overbudget, or even the manager with the best project management skills. The stories focus on two elements: the difference the manager made to their own development and the personal qualities of that manager. Reference will be made to the manager who:

- Provided challenge and enabled the individual to do things they did not believe they could do.
- Was willing to offer support.
- Recognized individual differences and worked with them.
- Trusted staff.
- Did not pretend that they knew everything.
- Listened.
- Gave honest feedback.
- Recognized the individual's strengths and gave them scope.

The qualities we recognize as having made a difference to our own performance, and that we remember in the best of our managers, are the qualities that are central to the STARTED coaching process. The ability to offer support and challenge to thinking. The ability to challenge and support the other person to do more, by accessing their own strengths and resources. A willingness to focus on the other person and not impose our own values and solutions. We value those managers who have used their skills to help us maximize our own contribution towards organizational objectives. We value them because they used their skills to help us remove the interference that gets in the way of performance: lack of confidence, the strong internal critic, fear of consequences, faulty assumptions.

As recipients of those qualities, we personally benefit, but the individual who can offer those qualities also benefits by showing that their capabilities extend beyond the disciplines of management into those of leadership. Daniel Goleman, a leading thinker on emotional intelligence, has written of the key role of the leader as the creator of resonance. By this he means the ability to create 'a reservoir of positivity that frees the best in people'.[2] Coaching is central to the creation of resonance because it connects what an individual wants to achieve with the organization's goals.

The power of coaching within a leader's skill set is that when staff can see that, allied to their leader's ability to provide a motivating vision, to set the pace in presenting challenges and their ability to provide clear direction, the leader is able to use empathy and rapport to help them raise their performance, the recipe is a powerful one for mutual success.

The evidence of this is seen in the performance of winning skippers in the BT Global Challenge Round the World Yacht Race.[3] In looking at the performance of podium skippers (skippers who occupied the top three places within a race leg) there were clear differences between them and those skippers who sat in the middle and back positions. All skippers showed evidence of management capabilities. To sail a vessel manned by a large group of individuals of very varying experience and skills safely around the world in race conditions calls on skills of resource management, conflict management, discipline and control. It requires that the skippers have a strong focus on performance and are highly self-motivating. The authors labelled this combination of skills and attributes 'Factor X'. All skippers possessed those skills and qualities, but podium skippers possessed them to a greater degree than teams who did not perform so well. Differentiation was equally marked on the skills and attributes labelled 'Factor Y'. Factor Y related to the ability of the skipper to be open, to be sensitive to the needs of the crew and to act with integrity. It required of the skipper that they could share leadership, give recognition and evidence a sense of belief in individuals. The more successful skippers allied Factor Y to a stronger focus on performance than was shown on less successful boats. They were able to link performance-driving (Factor X) to performance-enabling (Factor Y); using qualities central to effective coaching in enabling that performance to be delivered.

Those performance-enabling qualities were not inherent in the winning skippers. When tested for Emotional Intelligence[4] (EI) at the beginning of the race, the podium skippers performed less well than their competitors. When retested at the end of the race their EI scores were higher than the rest. It was found that in the process of living and working with a team in the closest of proximities for nine months, the application of EI skills such as awareness of others' needs and awareness of the impact they made on others, made a difference to performance; they learnt that the 'soft stuff' supported the 'hard stuff'. The skills used by the skippers to win out against the competition are skills that all effective coaches have. Equally important, the BT Global Challenge experience points to evidence that these qualities can be developed, and their development is helped when allied to a desire to raise performance.

CASE STUDY

Andrea was ambitious for a visible leadership role. She had been given clear feedback that, strong as her management skills were, they were insufficient for someone who wanted to inspire others. Central to the organization's reservations was her inability to motivate others to perform to their best. She relied on a strongly punitive model, where there was a regular application of the 'stick' but very little evidence of a reward 'carrot'. Through coaching, Andrea came to see that if she wanted to gain the willing commitment of others to self-manage their performance levels she needed to show that she could listen to staff, that she believed in their capability and that she was willing to help them do things their own way. For some while, Andrea sat in the contemplation position: recognizing there was some value in taking a different approach but equally convinced that people only do things when they are told what to do and how. When she decided to take action, she focused on new starters. She began her relationship with them testing out the ideas that she had intellectually accepted, but had no practical experience of applying. She found that by signalling both her expectations of performance and her willingness to offer support to help them find the best way of meeting those standards, the quality of both the output and her relationships with those staff was different. Buoyed up by success she gradually extended the range of staff with whom she applied this approach. She found that the risk of allying support with challenge and being more sensitive to others' needs, was outweighed by the rewards that came from doing so. A year later she could recognize the difference between management and leadership, in the confidence she now had that she could set direction and ensure that others would want to be part of contributing to achieving success.

The concern that Andrea had, a concern of many managers when introduced to the idea of using a coaching style to deliver results, is that it risks being an exercise with no measurable outcome. The reality, is that while a 'coaching style may not scream "bottom line" results, in a surprisingly indirect way, it delivers them'.[5]

What's the benefit for you?

For coaching to become integrated into your own management behaviours, and to justify the effort involved, you need to have a sense of the benefits that can accrue from developing that style. As one pragmatic manager said to me,

'Unless you can show me that it will make my staff do their jobs better without making them dependent on me, I will never coach'.

Ask yourself these questions:

- What do I believe that developing a coaching style can add to my present repertoire of management skills?
- What can the use of coaching enable me to do/achieve more effectively?
- What convinces me that it is worthwhile spending time coaching staff?
- What will developing my coaching skills get me?
- What form of scaffolding do I need to commit to coaching, and to take the risk of doing things differently?

The answer to those questions will shape the motivation that you take to the development of you as a leader through coaching.

Start small

The aim of applying the STARTED process is to make you a FAST coach: a manager who coaches as an embedded part of their conversations with staff. Once you start to listen with intent, it becomes inevitable that you will invite your staff to talk about their performance issues in a different way. Once you apply the STARTED framework your conversations will quickly focus on finding solutions to their difficulties and move away from the problem. However, as with any new behaviour, it will require practice; it will feel self-conscious at first:

- The instinct to ask 'Why?', and stopping yourself from doing so, will slow down thought processes.
- The selection of the right question that supports the purpose of the speaker rather than the curiosity of the listener, is hard work.
- The effort of listening for content that is above the waterline, and for the below-the-waterline information about the values and emotions they bring to the issue is tiring.
- The instinct to produce an answer for someone who is struggling can be overwhelming.
- To accept that you are not the expert can feel as though you are not adding value.

For all these reasons, it is important to start small. Begin with a problem that is not of central importance to the coachee's overall performance. Begin with the person in your team with whom you would feel most comfortable trying something new. Scale yourself on your confidence to coach your staff, and identify those things that will increase your confidence. Ensure that your early conversations do take place in a more formal environment and with time set aside, so that you do not feel exposed or rushed. The coaching conversation sitting on the corner of a desk that is completed in ten minutes may be your eventual target. In order to get there, you need to give time to embedding the behaviours until a solution focused way of addressing problems is so natural you don't even think about it.

As you build your coaching skills, look around you and notice the impact it has, not just on the individual who receives the coaching, but on the system around them. Your aim as a leader is to shape the culture in which you operate. Signalling your trust in the ability of others to raise their performance through their own self-knowledge and experience will enable them to do the same with their staff.

Former CEO of Manpower Ltd, Lance Secretan, has written of great leadership being about 'human experiences not processes'.[6] There is no experience at work more powerful than feeling that what you do matters. There is no more powerful enabler to performance than the attention of someone who wants you to be your best. As a manager you have the opportunity to make that difference, through your coaching. Get STARTED.

References

1. Herzberg, F., Mausner, B. and Snyderman, B. (1959) *The Motivation to Work.* Wiley.
2. Goleman, D., Boyatzis, R. and McKee, A. (2002) *The New Leaders.* Harvard Business Press, p. ix.
3. Cranwell-Ward, J., Bacon, A. and Mackie, R. (2002) *Inspiring Leadership: Staying Afloat in Turbulent Times.* Thomson.
4. Higgs, M. and Dulewicz, V. (1999) *Making Sense of Emotional Intelligence.* NFER-Nelson.
5. Goleman, D., Boyatzis, R. and McKee. A., *op cit.*, p. 63.
6. Secretan, L. (2004) *Inspire! What Great Leaders Do.* John Wiley and Sons.

Index